The Last Generation

ALAN ROBERTSON

CANADIAN CATALOGUING IN PUBLICATION DATA

Robertson, Alan, 1923–
    The last generation

ISBN 0-9688019-0-0

    1. Robertson, Alan, 1923– 2. World War, 1939–1945–Personal narratives, Canadian. 3. Great Britain. Royal Air Force—Biography. 4. World War, 1939-1945—Aerial operations, British.
D811.R62 2000   940.54'4941'092   C00911350-9

Cover illustration by John Hall
Design and Layout by Vancouver Desktop Publishing Centre Ltd.
Printed in Canada by Printcrafters

For information contact:
Sha-a-lan
P.O. Box 8712
Victoria, BC
v8w 3s3
Canada
oceanflyer@home.com

for my children
Clive and Penny,
Anne and Matthew,

and for their children,

and their children's children,

until the last generation

Contents

Foreword

IN THE PAST SIXTY YEARS many books have been published based upon the lives of those who, like myself, were profoundly affected by their experiences in World War II. So many, in fact, that one might ask oneself the question, why another?

My oldest son, Clive, was born six months after the war in Europe was over, and has no direct experience of the way in which our generation's responses to the war were conditioned by circumstances almost beyond our control, yet it is very much through his persistent urging that this book has been written. It is for this reason that I have dedicated it to my children.

I do this not with any high moral or philosophical aim that it will sway their judgement one way or another about the efficacy or futility of all wars, but merely to share with them, and the generations that follow them, how one individual in their family attempted to cope with the social upheaval that resulted from what some military historians refer to as The Last Great War.

—*Alan Robertson*
Vancouver, 2000

Acknowledgements

MANY PEOPLE HAVE HELPED me with this book, but I would particularly like to thank Roy Hayter for his perceptive first reading and his many useful suggestions; Patty Baldwin for her assistance in realising Roy's ideas concerning the thumbnail sketches; James Derham-Read and Bob Hall for their encouraging comments and supportive friendship; Richard Probert for his good example; and John Hall for understanding the boy that is within the man, for identifying with my love of the sea and the sky, and for conceptualising and producing a cover design that has so many layers of meaning.

I am grateful also to Linda Field for her editorial contributions which have kept me on track, and to Patty Osborne for steering me through the perils of publishing.

Finally, I would like to thank my dear wife, Shanna, for her unreserved encouragement and support, for assisting with the illustrations, and in helping in so many other ways to bring this project to a satisfying conclusion. Any shortcomings are entirely my own responsibility.

Chronology of Related Events

1923		Adolf Hitler's Beer Hall Putsch fails
1926		Benito Mussolini gains political power in Italy
1927		General Strike in Great Britain
1929		Stock Market crashes leading to Great Depression
1933		Franklin D. Roosevelt becomes President of U.S.A.
1935		Italy invades Ethiopia
1936		German propaganda film "Triumph of the Will" premieres at Nuremberg
1937		Japan invades China Adolf Hitler rises to power in Germany Spanish Civil War results in bombing of civilian targets
1938		Prime Minister Neville Chamberlain returns from Munich meeting with Hitler promising "peace in our time" Hitler takes over Austria
1939	31 Aug.	Hitler invades Poland
	3 Sep.	Britain and France declare war on Germany and Commonwealth Countries follow suit
1940	9 Apr.	Hitler invades Norway and Denmark
	10 May	Hitler invades the Netherlands

	21 May	Belgium and Luxembourg fall
	3 June	Germans bomb Paris
	10 June	British Expeditionary Force retreats from Dunkirk
1940	16 June	France surrenders
	7 Sep.	Blitz on London starts with the bombing of London's East End and docks
	13 Sep.	Buckingham Palace hit by bombs in daylight raid on London
	29 Dec.	Second Great Fire of London starts when more than 10,000 incendiary bombs fall on the city
1941	7 Dec.	Japanese attack U.S. Fleet at Pearl Harbor
	8 Dec.	Japan invades Hong Kong
1942	Feb.	Singapore falls to Japan
	19 Aug.	Allied raid on Dieppe results in Canada's losing two-thirds of its force
1943	May	Turning point in Battle of the Atlantic with forty-one U-boats destroyed and thirty-seven others damaged
1944	6 June	Operation Overlord: Allied invasion of Normandy
1945	2 May	Berlin falls and Axis forces in Italy surrender
	8 May	Victory in Europe—the war is officially over
	6 Aug.	First atom bomb dropped on Hiroshima killing 80,000 people
	10 Aug.	Second atom bomb dropped on Nagasaki killing 40,000 people
	2 Sep.	Formal surrender of Japan signed on the U.S. battleship Missouri in Tokyo Bay

Prologue

HE PUSHED THE STICK forward gently and the sleek little aircraft responded eagerly as it nosed over and descended into the low-flying area. He eased back the throttle to control the rising airspeed and took a quick look around to check his position. He could see the snow-covered shape of Boston Stump over to the south-east, and the familiar outline of Tattershall Castle ahead and to port. He made a spiral turn to port and starboard to check for other traffic and, once he was satisfied that all was clear, he brought the aircraft down to tree-top height. As he pulled the nose up over the trees that fringed the large meadow ahead, he felt the surge of excitement that comes with the sensation of increased speed. He eased the stick forward until the wheels were just skimming the snow. Everything was somehow clearer, larger than life. He zoomed over the next row of trees and came low over a field where a red fox was sitting in the open gateway, sniffing the cold morning air. As he pulled the aircraft around in a steep turn, he looked over his shoulder, trying to keep the fox in sight. He didn't feel the slight tremor on the controls. The fuselage began to vibrate, the nose pitched up and the whole aircraft yawed violently to the left. The port wing dropped suddenly, the wing tip sliced between the tree tops, the

aircraft continued to roll and struck the ground in an inverted position. The cockpit canopy plowed a deep black furrow in the soft white snow and the tailplane snapped off and bounced high in the air.

The Chipmunk trainer came to rest almost in the middle of the large fen and there was a moment of silence. Then, as fuel from a fractured pipe poured over the hot exhaust manifold, a hungry lick of orange flame engulfed the cockpit. The fire burned fiercely but briefly, and there remained only the ticking sound of cooling incandescent metal in the charred wreckage. It began to snow again.

◆ ◆ ◆

". . . We shall not all sleep, but we shall all be changed, in a moment, in the twinkling of an eye, at the last trump (for the trumpet shall sound), and the dead shall be raised incorruptible, and we shall be changed."

"Poor sod, he's certainly changed," I thought, as I looked at the flag-draped coffin where it rested on wooden trestles in front of the altar. Senses heightened by recollection, I became aware of the smell of damp serge uniforms that seemed to pervade every corner of the village church. I wondered how many knights and squires had been laid to rest in this tiny place of worship that had endured since the twelfth century. A battered helm hung from an iron hook embedded in one of the pillars, and a faded, tattered banner stirred overhead in the slight draft, a reminder of the ghosts of warriors young and old.

Today the old church was filled with Hardy's fellow cadets, here to pay their last respects.

"Death is swallowed up in victory. O Death, Where is thy sting? O grave, where is thy victory?"

The Chaplain had concluded the funeral service with a Lesson from the Epistle of Paul to the Corinthians, and then led the solemn procession into the churchyard.

The pallbearers gently laid the casket to rest on the webbing straps that would lower the coffin into the newly-prepared grave. A cold wind whipped through the ranks of the mourners, and I glanced over to where a frail couple in their fifties stood looking blankly at their son's last resting place.

"Man that is born of woman hath but a short time to live, and is full of misery. He cometh up, and is cut down, like a flower; he fleeth as it were a shadow."

Mr. Hardy had been stoic and controlled as we stood looking out over the parade ground. "She's taken this very hard, Flight Lieutenant, you see, he's our only child." He paused to take a careful sip of sherry, seeking to give voice to something that troubled him. "Everyone's been extremely kind, but do you think . . . I mean, could you possibly tell me . . . I was wondering if. . . ." His voice faltered. Then he straightened his bowed shoulders and

continued more firmly: "Can you tell me if our boy suffered . . . at the end, I mean. Or was he. . . ." I thought of my own eight-year-old son I had left an hour ago, safe and happy, playing with his toys in the peaceful garden of our home and I felt something of the older man's pain, and shook my head. I thought for a moment, searching for the right words of comfort.

"No, Mr. Hardy, death was instantaneous. He wouldn't have felt a thing." I gently placed my hand on his arm. "I know—it's small comfort to you right now, but I believe he died doing something he wanted to do more than anything else in the world. I was the last one to speak to him before he took off, and I know how eager he was to be in the air again." The sound of earth falling on the coffin brought me back to the present moment.

"Foreasmuch as it hath pleased Almighty God of his great mercy to take unto himself our dear brother here departed, we therefore commit his body to the ground; earth to earth, ashes to ashes, dust to dust."

A flight of Vampire jets whistled overhead in the 'finger four' formation honouring a missing or fallen comrade. The guard of honour fired a volley of rifle fire that shattered the peace of the countryside. A startled flock of ragged crows fluttered from the copse at the end of the churchyard, their raucous cries a harsh antiphony to the crashing thunder of the RAF's final salute to the dead pilot. The College Trumpeter stepped forward and raised the silver instrument to his lips. I usually managed to control my emotions on these occasions, but as the notes of the Last Post pierced the wintry air, I felt hot tears welling up and rolling down my cheeks.

I swallowed to ease the ache in my throat. Memories of the long ago are still painful. Intellectually, I can understand that grief is a cleansing, healing process. I accept that. But I also know something deep inside, something that only life experience can teach. Even if learning is painful, it should never be joyless. It should always move the human spirit forward.

Prelude to War

THE RAGGED LINE OF KHAKI-CLAD figures toiled up the steep slope, sweating and panting in the mid-day sun, rifles at the ready, safety catches off. The men crested a fold in the chalk downs, possibly a sheep track, and looked to me as their section leader to halt or go on to the summit nearly 500 feet above us. Despite the lance-corporal's single stripe on my sleeve, I was uncertain what to do. If we stopped here we would be in dead ground, sheltered from hostile fire, but we would be unable to spot the enemy's position.

"A Gordon for me!" The cry rang out from above, to be echoed immediately by a chorus of fierce yells and a volley of rifle fire. My indecision vanished and I yelled, "Take cover." The well-rehearsed firing order followed: "Number 1 Section, open sights, five rounds rapid. Fire!"

I made a tripod with my elbows on the bank, spread my legs, and pulled the butt of my Short Lee Enfield rifle snugly into my shoulder. I looked along the vee of the aperture sight and raised the foresight carefully into position, waiting for a target of opportunity. I took up the first pressure on the trigger.

A skirl of bagpipes wailed from the top of the hill, and then a thin line of bonneted and kilted figures crested the rise and

The Pennings O.T.C. Camp, Tidworth.

began a steady advance down the slope, rifles at the low cant, white gaiters moving in rhythm. I took careful aim at the leading man, a corporal, and squeezed off five rounds in quick succession. On either side of me the rest of the section were pushing fresh clips of cartridges into their rifles.

"Fix bayonets. Charge!"

There was a glint of silver as bayonets were snapped into place, then came a chorus of murderous screams as the line came thundering down towards our position. On my left, Pete Spencer rose to his knees and fumbled to get a quick shot at his opponent, but was knocked flat by a burly Scot who deftly parried his rifle barrel, firing at the same time. Pete screamed in agony and dropped to the ground, clutching his arm to his side.

"Did ye think we were playin' games, wee laddie?" The highlander lowered his bayonet until it rested on Pete's chest. "In war ye play for keeps." Then he laughed. "Ye'll remember your first brush with the King's Own Scottish Borderers, won't you, laddie? Now let's tak' a look at your arm.

18

He knelt beside Pete and gently rolled back the sleeve to reveal a painful-looking powder burn. Pete stared up at him, the colour draining from his face, lips trembling, fighting to keep the tears back. The highlander took a field dressing from his tunic and deftly bandaged Pete's wrist.

"This your section, Corporal? Looks like ye have your first casualty. Better send him back to the First Aid Post before his arm blisters. And if ye don't mind a bit of advice, ye'll give the order to fix bayonets next time ye're attacking a position that's atop a hill. Best to be prepared for what ye canna see." Then he winked and strode off down the hill.

"Your chaps all right, Corporal?" A red-tabbed officer wearing an umpire's white armband came puffing up the slope. "Jolly good show. Saw how your fellas faced the Kosbies without flinchin'. That's the stuff. Made good use of cover and kept your heads. Heard your fire order loud and clear from my position in those trees. Gave you good marks for stickin' to your guns. What's your name, Corporal? This chap goin' to be all right?"

I saluted smartly. "Lance-Corporal Robertson, Wilson's OTC. He's all right, sir. Just a powder burn. I'm sending him back to First Aid for treatment."

"Might as well take the whole section back now. Your battalion's reached its objective and your company's regrouping at the bivouac area. I expect your fellows could do with a good cuppa char. You, too, eh Corporal? Damned fine show, chaps!" And with a cheery wave of his swagger stick, he strode off.

"You all right, Pete? Can you make it back with us, or shall I send for the stretcher bearers?" I picked up his rifle and slung it over my shoulder.

Pete looked at the anxious faces of his mates in Number 1 Section, then grinned as he scrambled to his feet. "Not a chance," he said. "I'll make it back on my own two feet. Piece of cake."

It was the summer of 1938. I was in the fourth form at grammar school, and had just celebrated my fifteenth birthday before coming to the OTC Summer Camp at Tidworth Pennings on Salisbury Plain. At the end of the spring term, I had passed the Certificate 'A' Examination, and knew that my name would be placed on the Supplementary List of Reserve Officers on my sixteenth birthday. Like most of my school chums, I was absolutely confident of Britain's military supremacy, but trustingly naive in my belief in Neville Chamberlain's promise of 'peace in our time.' Nevertheless, it was impossible not to be aware of the preparations being made for war, a war that our parents did not want, but a reality they accepted with both a firm resolve and a willingness to meet with practical measures.

Although I was unaware of it at the time, two of my youthful experiences were to have a far-reaching influence on my future. One was my OTC training and the other was my service as a volunteer with the London Auxiliary Fire Service. All through the autumn and winter of 1938, and into the spring and summer of 1939, I attended weekly training sessions at the Gresham Road, Brixton, Fire Station, and at the London Fire Brigade's Headquarters on the Albert Embankment. I was recruited as a messenger/dispatch rider, together with my 98 cc Coventry-Eagle two-stroke motorcycle. Britain's Civil Defence Plan in 1938 was heavily influenced by London's experience of Zeppelin raids during the Great War of 1914-18.

Accordingly, our training was predicated on the belief that air-raids on London might be expected even before a formal declaration of war was made. The classes were thorough and comprehensive, and included foot drill (a legacy from the Royal Navy), semaphore signalling, hose drill, and the operation of the powerful Coventry-Climax trailer pumps that were to be towed behind requisitioned taxi-cabs. It was a physically demanding program and, for a sixteen-year-old, rather daunting—especially the ladder-training, which involved scaling a sixty-foot tower with a fifteen-foot hook-ladder. At the completion of our training, we were assigned to crews of six, consisting of a sub-officer, three firemen, a telegraphist (usually a retired post office worker in his late sixties), and a young messenger with his bicycle or small motorcycle. The wartime operational plan was to disperse individual crews with their fire appliances at strategic points in the local fire district, with the hope that, in the event of a direct bomb hit on a fire station, the surviving resources would be sufficient to continue fighting fires in the local area.

On Thursday, August 31, 1939, the BBC six o'clock news broadcast announced a general mobilisation of all Civil Defence personnel, and I donned my uniform and reported for duty. I was told to fill my fuel tank and was given a list of names and addresses of those auxiliary firemen who had not yet reported. An immediate blackout was in effect, and I set off with an improvised mask over my headlamp. Apart from brief halts to refuel and grab a sandwich from the station canteen, I rode all through Friday and Saturday until an officer, noticing my weariness, told me to bed down for a few hours on a mattress in the corridor. I awoke to hear my name being called by that same officer, assigning me and my crew to a fire alarm under the railway bridge at Loughborough Junction, close to my home.

The crew clambered into the taxi in full fire-fighting gear. Sub-Officer Chevalier stood impressively on the running board, one hand on the roof rack, the other on the shiny, new brass bell, and taxi and trailer-pump drove sedately out of the station yard. I followed at a respectful distance on my motorbike.

Our assigned post was in a builder's yard snuggled under the arches of a railway viaduct, and the owner met us at the gate, dressed in the full battle order of the Royal West Kent Regiment, Territorial Army.

As he handed over his keys, he said, "Make yourselves at home, mates. I'm off to join my unit at Catford. Got to show this 'itler feller 'e can't get away with murder. Probably be 'ome by Christmas. Well, good luck then." And he marched off briskly, with his kitbag on one shoulder and his Short Lee Enfield rifle slung easily on the other. The crew wasted no time in getting the vehicles under cover, then lined up smartly awaiting further instructions. The sub-officer ordered the crew to stow their gear in the builder's mess hall, then he sat down on the taxi's running board and deliberately filled and lit his pipe before turning to me.

"Sit down, lad," he said kindly. "How're you feeling? Are you frightened?"

"I don't think so, sir. Do you think they'll bomb us tonight?"

"Shouldn't think so, though it's hard to say from what little I know. We've just been ordered to stand to and to await further orders. That's where you come in. You'll ride to the station at 09:00 hours each day for routine orders, but you'll also have to act as our cook. I've talked it over with the other lads, and we've agreed that each man will put in a shilling a day for messing. D'ye think you can give us three good meals a day for six bob? I'll put in for you until we get paid. Now, here's seven and six. Nip down to the junction and see what you can scrounge up for tomorrow's meals. Perhaps you'd better pick up six meat pies and six penn'oth of chips for supper tonight. Oh, and don't forget to buy some tea, sugar, and milk. The lads'll look forward to a nice cuppa when you get back. Take your bike, and don't forget your gas mask."

As I wheeled out of the yard, a confusion of thoughts ran through my mind. How was I going to cook three meals a day for six shillings? Why did the sub-officer tell me to take my gas mask? Supposing the air-raid sirens went while I was away from the post? I made a quick decision and went straight over the crossroads and headed for home. I hadn't seen my mother since Thursday, but she didn't seem too surprised to see me and soon gave me the advice I needed.

"Shop daily and plan three meals ahead. He's right, pies and chips'll do for tonight, but you'd better stock up for tomorrow. I'll give you some potatoes and a loaf of bread from the larder, and you'd better take my packet of Bisto to make gravy. Now, get some thick rashers of bacon from the butcher, and ask him for some stewing steak and beef kidneys for tomorrow's dinner. Fill them up with a nice sweet, trifle is easy to make, you can take those sponge fingers and some of Grandma's plum and apple jam. Take my box of Bird's custard, there's a recipe for trifle on the back. Oh, and here's a packet of raspberry jelly. Don't forget to make it tonight so's it'll be set by the morning. Better get six eggs for breakfast, they'll expect something special for Sunday morning. Don't look so worried. You can do it. We all have to start somewhere."

I thanked her, gave her a quick kiss, and made off with my carrier bag of supplies. My shopping expedition was a great success, and our family butcher gave me a pound of sausages to add to my store. By the time I'd stopped at Sainsbury's for butter, tea, sugar, flour, and milk, and had bought some fruit and vegetables at the market, I was surprised to find I still had sixpence left.

When I got back it was nearly dark, and the crew was sitting in the small kitchen which was to serve as our messroom for the next three months. A big black iron kettle was steaming away on the gas stove, and I made a large canteen of tea while the crew tucked into their meat pies and chips.

"What's for pudding?" asked the telegraphist, winking at the others as he helped me pass around mugs of tea.

I grinned back at him. "There's a bag of jam doughnuts and day-old pastries I got from the baker's next door. There's enough for two apiece. Cost a penny."

"Good for you, lad," said Chevalier, "I knew you could do it.

Now, the rest of you help young Robbie with the washing-up. He's doing the shopping and cooking, but he shouldn't have to do everything by himself."

He turned back to me. "We'll have breakfast at seven, so you'll have to be moving by six. Better doss down on that old sofa for the night. You've earned your rest. You'll find plenty of blankets in the fire appliance." He meant our taxi-cum-fire engine, of course.

Chevalier was a good officer, having served in the Royal Navy as a Chief Petty Officer. He knew all about duty rosters and establishing normal routines. He divided the night into two-hour watches and took the first trick himself. He had the telegraphist maintain an occurence book (he put the emphasis on the first syllable, 'OCK-rance') and, by his example, gave us all a feeling of hope which we sorely needed, and the confidence that our untried capabilities would be able to meet whatever the morrow brought.

I was up half an hour before six, splashing cold water on my face in the kitchen sink. My mind was racing ahead, planning the sequence of preparations for breakfast. I knew how much the crew was looking forward to a hearty meal and I didn't want to let them down. I had lit the gas under the big kettle when I got out of bed and it was soon on the boil. When the tea had steeped for three minutes, I poured out five mugs and laced them with a spoonful of condensed milk. Mo, the telegraphist, was on watch and he came over and picked up the tray.

"You get on with breakfast, lad, and I'll pass these around. Sing out if you need any help."

I was already busy with the cast iron frying pan, separating the fat, juicy rashers with a kitchen fork. While the rich smell of cooking bacon filled the kitchen, the crew was washing in the stone sink, having slept fully-clothed, removing only their rubber boots, in order to be ready for a quick turn out. I decided to scramble the eggs rather than attempt to serve them to order. I mixed in a little chopped onion and a little milk and seasoned the mixture with salt and pepper, as I'd seen my father do many times before, and cut a half-dozen thick slices of bread to fry in the bacon fat. I popped the bacon and fried bread in the oven on an enamel plate to keep warm, then emptied the egg mixture into the hot pan. Just as I'd finished filling the plates with bacon, fried bread, and scrambled eggs, the sub-officer appeared in the doorway with a bag of fresh crusty rolls from the bakery, together with a seven pound tin of strawberry jam.

"We're in luck, boys. The baker starts baking at four every morning, and he's going to set out a couple of loaves for us, to-gether with any left-over pastries. And by the look of this table, young Robbie'll not let us starve. Now get stuck in, everyone. Inspection at eight, pump drill at nine, and make do and mend at ten. Mo and Robbie can make a start at sandbagging the fire alarm post on the corner. There's plenty of clean sand and gravel in the yard, and the hose lorry has just dropped off a bale of sandbags. Robbie, you'll have to cut back here at ten-thirty and make a pail of tea before you start on dinner. We can all lis-ten to the BBC eleven o'clock news while we have our tea break."

By ten o'clock Mo and I had built a solid revetment of sand-bags around the fire alarm post. Mo had spent four years in the trenches in the first World War and what he didn't know about building dugouts was not worth knowing. He showed me how to alternate the courses so that the joins were never in line, and how to lay a couple of planks between layers to serve as seats and a

shelf. The entrance was designed with a dog leg so that whoever was inside would be protected from stray shrapnel and bomb blast. Three planks capped the structure with a couple of layers of sandbags on top for extra protection. Since the fire alarm post was sheltered by a railway bridge, there would be adequate protection from all but a direct hit. The final touch was added when Mo found a twenty-gallon drum to serve as a coke brazier. He had done the occasional stint as a nightwatchman when he retired, and he knew how to keep his old bones warm through the damp winter nights.

"All we need now, lad, is our own little tea pail 'ere and we can brew up our own char." He knocked his pipe out and nodded contentedly. "A good morning's work, young Robbie. Now let's get back to the yard and get that bucket o' tea made. I'll bet the lads are ready for a break."

Sipping large mugs of hot, sweet tea, we crowded around the Phillips wireless to hear the news. We listened in silence to Prime Minister Chamberlain's thin reedy voice pronouncing: ". . . I have received no such assurance . . . and I have to tell you that this country is now at war with Germany."

Chevalier stood up and switched off the set. "Right, lads. To your posts. Helmets and gas masks. Driver and crew at the ready. Mo, take up your post at the fire alarm, report in to the station, and start a listening watch. Robbie, nip on your bike and get down to the station right away and report for orders. Look sharp everyone."

I swung on the kickstarter and the two-stroke caught first time. As I wheeled out the gate and turned under the bridge in the direction of Gresham Road, the air-raid alert sounded. There was a siren at the corner of Shakespeare Road and wave upon wave of sound wailed in my ears. I looked up at the sky and saw the barrage balloons being raised on their cables, and I wondered if I'd reach the fire station before the first bomb fell.

Shaping Begins

R EPORTING TO RAF Station Cardington was an auspicious way to begin a new year. 1940 had been frustrating for me in many ways. The phony war had dragged on past that first Christmas that many had thought would see victory achieved. The remnants of the battered British Army were salvaged from the beaches of Dunkirk. At home, the restrictions brought about by the conflict began to irk, and across the English Channel the fall of France was the beginning of a long line of reverses that were to erode the optimism we all had felt in 1939.

It seemed right, somehow, to take some positive action. I had spoken to my father just before Christmas about the possibility of my joining the RAF. I asked him about his service during the Great War (we had not started to refer to our war as World War II yet), and learned that he had volunteered for the London Territorial Army, or the Terriers as he called it, at the age of fifteen-and-a-half. I got the impression that he didn't consider seventeen-and-a-half too young to enlist so I took the plunge on Boxing Day, added a year to my age, and was accepted for immediate service as a pilot with orders to report for duty on New Year's Day of 1941.

Cardington was an old RFC airfield noteworthy for its giant

airship hangars built to house the dirigibles that were Britain's answer to Count von Zeppelin's contribution to military aviation in the 1914-1918 War. As we marched about the camp, these mammoth hangars dominated our lives.

My stay at Cardington was brief but eventful. We had less than a week to be kitted out and inoculated against typhus, tetanus, and smallpox before being shipped off for recruit training. I found myself sharing a Nissen hut with twenty-three other recruits. Our temporary home was equipped with twenty-four iron cots and a coal-burning stove. The linoleum floor had been burnished to a high sheen by successive squads of new recruits and the pot-bellied stove gleamed with countless coats of blacking. As we stood to attention by our beds, we were told that we were expected to leave our hut in the same immaculate condition in which we found it. No one told us how, or with what, but necessity being the mother of invention our parents had told us about, it didn't take us long to find a way to share our new-found responsibilities and to organize work parties to deal with the challenge. By the time we left, my previous training and experience in the OTC and the London Fire Brigade had been recognised, and I marched proudly at the head of my squad as we set off for the railway station.

Our gentle treatment at Cardington ill-prepared us for our reception at RAF Station Bridgenorth, a small market down near the Welsh Border. Sergeant Todd was only five foot three, but what he lacked in stature he made up for in force of character. Like most drill sergeants he was well-versed in the psychology of motivation. His first move to establish control over us came when we tumbled off the train at six a.m. after an interminably long overnight journey from Bedfordshire to Shropshire. His crisp bark addressed us as we sleepily straggled into the station yard.

"Get fell in you dozy lot. Line up in three ranks, tallest on the right, shortest on the left. Right dress. When I call out your name, shout Sergeant, and don't mumble."

He consulted his clipboard and started to read the names of our intake alphabetically. "Adams, Alcock, Barker, Bird, Brown. . . ." He got us far as Meredith, which he pronounced in the Welsh manner (Me-RED-ith). There was no answer, so he repeated himself a few decibels louder. No answer.

He screamed at the top of his voice and his face turned a bright purple.

"I know you're 'ere somewhere, cos you got on the train at Cardington. Let's 'ave you then, Me-RED-ith. or I'll 'ave your guts for garters."

A tall, gangly and bespectacled young man dressed in corduroys, tweed jacket and college scarf, standing at the right of the front file, spoke up: "Excuse me, sir, but my name is pronounced ME-re-dith. I didn't know you were speaking to me."

Sergeant Todd strutted across the yard and stood looking up at Meredith. A silence endured for at least thirty seconds while the rest of us stood stiffly to attention like tightly coiled springs, fearful of the fate that awaited Meredith.

"Did you 'ear me, son? I'm not a sir, I'm a sergeant. And I don't want your family 'istory, I wants to 'ear you're 'ere. Now, let's 'ear you."

Meredith was awkward, but not stupid. He bellowed, "Sergeant!"

Todd looked at him for another thirty seconds, then marched briskly back to his position facing the squad and finished the roll call without further interruption.

"Squad! Kitbags on the left shoulder, riiiiiight turn! As you were."

He stalked over to stand in front of Meredith again, looking up into his face as if searching for some explanation to a deep mystery. Meredith had his kitbag over his right shoulder and had turned left. Todd looked at Meredith for a moment, then said: "You're a proper Charlie, aren't you, son. I meant your *other* left and your *other* right. Got it?"

Meredith hastily tranferred his kitbag to his left shoulder and, looking straight ahead, shouted, "Sergeant!"

Sergeant Todd marched back to his position and started again: "Squad! Right turn! By the left, quick march!"

We wheeled out of the station yard and started down the slope through the town, slipping and sliding on the frosty street.

"Dig those 'eels in 'ard. Swing your arms from the shoulder, arms straight, 'eads up and chests out. You're in the Royal Air Force now, be proud of it!"

It was three miles to RAF Station Bridgenorth, and by the time we marched past the guardhouse an hour later we were all sweating like cart horses. All except Sergeant Todd. Of course, he was only carrying a clipboard and we were wearing full marching order: webbing harness with back pack, haversack, water bottle, gas mask, steel helmet, and wearing our greatcoats and carrying our kit bags, with all our worldly possessions on our backs. We halted in front of our home for the next six weeks. Another Nissen hut.

"Facing front, left turn! Stand at ease! When I say Squad, brace yourselves, and when I dismiss you, turn right smartly, pause, and break ranks. Then find yourselves a bed inside the 'ut and stand at ease by your beds 'olding your kitbag at your left side. Squad! As you were! I said brace yourselves. Squad! Ah-ten-shun! Diiiss-miiiss!"

We tumbled up the steps, jostling for position, and I found myself looking for a bed near the potbellied stove in the centre of the hut. Two new friends I had met at Cardington beckoned me over and I just reached my place when Sergeant Todd entered the hut.

"Stand by your beds!"

We hastily assumed the position which was to become a frequent part of our lives in the following weeks for rollcalls, kit inspections and FFIs. The acronym was short for 'free from infection,' but it was more picturesquely referred to by the recruits as 'a short arm inspection.' The procedure had its comic moments. We would be standing easy by our beds and as soon as the Medical Officer had reached the next hut we were called to attention by Sergeant Todd. The MO stopped by each man who dropped his pants so that the penis could be inspected for any evidence of venereal diseases. The MO would lift the penis with his pencil and inspect the scrotum. On one occasion the MO stooped down to get a closer view and said, "What's your name?"

"Prosser, sir."

"How long have you had this?"

"D'ye mean the ball, sir?"

"Yes. How'd you get it?"

The rest of the hut stood rigidly to attention in an embarrassed silence.

Prosser broke the silent speculations. "I 'ad the mumps, sir, and it swole up and never went down."

The MO grunted. "Hmm, must be bloody awkward. We'll have to get you a truss. Report sick tomorrow morning and we'll get you fixed up." And with that he removed his pencil and moved on to the next set of appendages.

Prosser was just one of the delightful characters in our hut. He was a printer by trade, as well as a hot banjo player. He entertained us each evening as we blancoed our webbing and polished our brass. His favourite tune was an impressive arrangement of "Nola," and whenever I hear the tune on a local radio station's Golden Oldie program I invariably remember Prosser and his swollen ball.

Then there was Al Mahy, an eighteen-year-old British Latin American Volunteer from Buenos Aires. This energetic and enterprising Lothario had the most amazing sexual feats to describe whenever he came back from a Saturday night visit to Bridgenorth. Since most of us of his age were totally inexperienced in the facts of life, we listened to his exploits with incredulity. One Sunday morning he told us he'd had his way with a local lass on top of a mausoleum in a local cemetery. It had been a frosty night, but we believed him because he was a loner and there were no witnesses to contradict him.

Meredith was also a loner and was the squad's eccentric academic. He'd read foreign languages at Oxford, and eventually ended up working in Intelligence with Jugoslavia's General Tito. But at Bridgenorth he was a misfit in every sense of the word. His height and build had baffled the stores sergeant and the only items of clothing that could be found to fit him were his field cap and his size fourteen boots. Between these two extremities he was clad as an undergraduate student and presented a most incongruous figure on the parade ground. We loved him because he was the bane of Sergeant Todd's life. He never took to marching drill and barely managed to distinguish left from right until just before our graduation parade.

My two close friends were Johnny and Farmer, who were both twenty-one and eminently suitable mentors for a seventeen-year-old who hadn't completed secondary school. They were totally different.

Johnny was a sophisticated young man of the world, a bit of a playboy, with his own apartment in Bristol and a string of girlfriends from the middle class society he came from. Whenever we had a weekend pass, Johnny's parents entertained Farmer and I in their comfortable surburban home in Watford.

His teenage sister worshipped him and we shared some of his reflected glory as pilots-in-training.

Farmer was a different breed entirely. Born and raised not too far from Bridgenorth, he was from Shrewsbury, the shire town of Shropshire. He was deliberate and slow of speech with the soft burr of the countryside. He was a model of routine and took to recruit training with a philosophic acceptance of his new life. He had matriculated from grammar school and had already started on a career with the local council that was to be merely interrupted by his wartime service in the RAF. Like James Herriot, the veterinary doctor from Yorkshire who later became a successful author, he had a firm idea of where he was going. He served with distinction as a torpedo bomber pilot in Coastal Command and returned after the war to become a loyal and respected servant of the County Council.

These two good friends were my constant companions for over a year and much of my maturing from schoolboy to manhood I owe to them both. We shared many new and exciting experiences and enjoyed that kind of comradeship that leaves its footprint forever imprinted on each other's souls.

I was the youngest and, thanks largely to their support and encouragement, I was the first to go solo. We were inseparable and supported each other through those early days of recruit training and it was with a great deal of pride that we marched together at the passing out parade that marked our emergence as Aircraftsmen 2nd Class (General Duties), or 'erks' as we were known, and our feet placed on the lowest rung of the ladder that could ultimately lead to the rank of Marshal of the Royal Air Force.

THREE

General Duties

O<small>UR NEXT MOVE WAS TO</small> Number 11 Operational Training Unit (Bomber Command) at Bassingbourn in Cambridgeshire, where we really learned what the General Duties Branch was all about. It was the category that all aircrew came under, but it also included all the other non-specialised officers and airmen except those in the technical and the equipment and supply branches.

We were ordered to report to the Station Warrant Officer, Mr. Haynes, or Hoppy as he was known behind his back (never to his face!), either because of the leg injury he had received in the Great War, or because of his habit of hopping into view just when you were doing something you shouldn't, like taking a short cut across the parade square, sacred ground to Mr. Haynes. His voice could stop a wayward airman dead in his tracks at a thousand yards. He had merely to emerge from his office in the Administration building and bellow, "You, airman!" to have every 'erk' within audible range march smartly to attention just in case he was the guilty party.

Farmer, Johnny and I stood to attention in his office while he surveyed with evident distaste the white flashes in our caps that denoted pilots-in-training. "U/T Pilots, are you? Well, you can report to the Flying Wing Flight Sergeant in Hangar Number Three. Look sharp!"

We were buzzing with excitement as we marched to the airfield where we could see several twin-engined Wellington bombers (nicknamed Wimpies).

We had visions of the Air Ministry's having recognised our potential and of allowing us to skip elementary flying training and go straight on to operational flying. We weaved our way through the third hangar between Wimpies in various stages of inspection or repair, revelling in the smell of hydraulic fluid, engine oil, and aviation petrol. Flight Sergeant Fielding's office was up a flight of stairs overlooking the hangar floor and next to the Wing Commander Flying. He quickly shattered our illusions when he assigned us to each of the three flight commanders.

"Your duties are to keep the flight commander's office and the crew rooms clean at all times. I'll be through the flights every morning at 09:00 hours and I want to see the place spotless. Also it's your duty to see the flight commander's fire is laid and lit before he comes in, so you'll have to be on the job by 08:00. Now cut along and report to your flights."

'C' Flight Commander, Flight Lieutenant Hudson, DFC, was a kindly man in his early twenties who told me to stand at ease and asked me some personal question about my school and the sports I'd played. He appeared genuinely interested in my replies and asked me if I understood my duties and if I had any questions about the job.

"Sir, how long will it be before we start our flying training and is there any chance of getting some air experience?"

"Afraid I've no idea how long it'll be, but as long as you do your job here there's no reason why you shouldn't fly as much as you like. Ask any of the instructors and they'll tell you where to pick up a helmet and parachute."

The flying instructors were equally accommodating and we found that our cleaning duties didn't prevent us from flying both day and night. We usually went up with an instructor and his student, and were able to stand between the pilots' seats and look over their shoulders, or, once we were airborne, to lie in the bomb aimer's position looking out of the nose turret. At that time, in the early spring of 1941, the principal hazards (apart from flying with inexperienced bomber pilots) were the weather in south-east England, and the sudden appearance of enemy intruders in the circuit, usually at night, and in the form of twin-engined Junker's 88s.

The German pilots' technique was to follow a Wellington in on the final approach to the flarepath and as soon as its wheels and flaps came down to fire a long burst of cannon fire from close range. During the first two weeks I was at Bassingbourn we lost three aircraft to night intruders and, because I was a strapping young lad, I was called upon to act as pall bearer at no less than seven funerals in a week. As I carried the coffins I wondered how much of the bodies were left to bury. However, these thoughts didn't seem to curb my eagerness to fly as much as possible.

The other hazard we had to face was the unpredictable level of skill of the student pilots we flew with. One cloudy afternoon I was watching a Wellington on the approach to land when, even to my inexpert eye, it was evident that the aircraft was on the point of stalling as the pilot stretched his glide to reach the threshold of the field. I recalled the dictum of one of

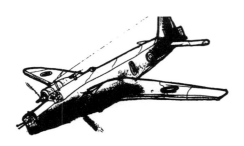

our flight-sergeant flying instructors, 'When in doubt, go around again.'

When I saw that the aircraft was going to crash, I ran into the flight commander's office and he was on his feet in a second, racing out to his little Hillman van and yelling to me to follow. We bumped across the grass to the burning wreck and he grabbed a fire-axe from the cab and started to hack away at the canvas-covered geodetic fuselage. We could see through the flame and the smoke that the two pilots were still alive and crawling toward the rear exit. Flight Lieutenant Hudson grabbed an arm and called out for me to help him. I reached into the fuselage and caught hold of a leg from which all clothing had burnt away. I gave a great heave and the leg came away in my hand and I fell back on the grass.

"Get back to the truck. Clear out! *Now!*" We just made it to the Hillman when the tanks blew with a great blast of hot air. "Jump in, we're too late to help them. The crash truck and ambulance are here." As we drove away, a shroud of snow-white foam extinguished the flames, and covered the charred wreckage and the corpses of the two pilots.

It all happened so quickly that I hadn't noticed that the sleeve of my battle dress tunic was singed, or that the hairs on my wrists had turned into grey powder.

"Get yourself a parachute and harness and a spare helmet. You're coming up with me in 'C' Charlie."

I looked at the Flight Commander in a daze, uncomprehending.

"Look lively, you clot. We haven't got all day," and he turned away to his office.

I threw a parachute over my shoulder, picked up a spare helmet and ran out to join him. He was already strapping himself into the left-hand seat and pointed to the co-pilot's position. "We're going to do an air test. They've just finished a minor inspection and I want to check the trim controls."

He gave the groundcrew a thumbs up sign and started the port engine. Once it had fired and was idling steadily, he started the starboard engine. While both Pegasus engines were warming up he called out the pre-taxi check list, pointing to each item as he did: "Brake pressure . . . hydraulic pressure . . . hatches closed . . . all clear to taxi." He called for taxi clearance, waved away the chocks, and turned on to the perimeter track. Reaching the take-off point, he parked at forty-five degrees to the direction of the wind and completed the pre-take-off check. Receiving a green signal from the Duty Pilot in the Air Traffic Control caravan he turned into wind on the wire mesh netting and opened the throttles wide. The Wimpy lumbered across the airfield until the tail came up and we gained flying speed. Then he eased back on the control column gently and we were airborne and climbing away to the northeast. At 3,000 feet he levelled off and satisfied himself that both rudder and elevator trim controls were working smoothly. He spoke on the intercom: "Put your hands and feet lightly on the controls and follow me through. See where the nose is in relation to the horizon. Look at the VSI and notice where the needle is centred. Check the altimeter, steady at 3,000 feet. Wings parallel to the horizon. We're flying straight and level. Feel it? Good, you have control."

I realised with a rush of joy that for the first time in my life I was flying an aircraft. This is what I'd joined the RAF to do. This is what the recruiting poster was all about with its message: "There's a Spitfire or a Wellington waiting for you!"

"Hold the control column lightly. Now turn the wheel gently to port, to the left. A slight backward pressure at the same time. There, you're turning to port, well done. Now turn the wheel the other way and relax the backward pressure, and as soon as the wings are level return the wheel to the centre.

"There, you're flying straight and level again. Now try a turn to starboard.

"Watch the nose doesn't drop, and add a light touch of right rudder. Good, hold it here for a moment. Well done, now straighten out again. Good for you, Robertson. Here endeth the first lesson. I have control," and he put his hands back on the wheel.

He put the wheel hard over and thrust the control column forward, taking the aircraft down into a long winding turn until we were scudding over the fens at 150 feet. He looked over to check my reaction and grinned when he saw that I was eagerly leaning forward against the harness.

"Ever see King's Lynn?" he asked. I shook my head and gasped as he took the Wimpy down to fifty feet. We came to the end of the fen and he gently eased the aircraft up over the trees and down to the deck on the other side. As we neared the market town he climbed up to 500 feet and levelled off.

"What the hell's going on? Cheeky bastards. Jerry's raiding the town in broad daylight. Those are Heinkel 111's coming in from the east. Looks like they're making for the airfield. See, they're raising the barrage balloons and the ack-ack is getting their range. No place for an unarmed Wimpy to be hanging around. Let's beetle off home and get back on the ground before they notice us and get the wrong idea. Discretion is the better part of valour in our case. Hold tight!"

As we ran for home I knew that he'd wanted to take my mind off the crash.

A little more than six months before, I had seen the first daylight raid on London from a vantage point on the railway viaduct at Peckham Rye Station, and remembered watching the raid develop with a feeling of disbelief. Yes, we had all been prepared for air raids by night, but not for the long period of the phony war when the warning sirens were invariably a false alarm and the All Clear was sounded within a matter of minutes. The problem for Londoners was that with every false alarm the possibility of an air raid became increasingly remote and unthinkable. All that had changed in August 1940 when the sirens sounded and a Red Alert was signalled by the Civil Defence authorities in South London.

I was waiting on the platform for a train to take me home to Streatham Common when a great armada of German bombers and fighters flew steadily up the Thames estuary towards the East End of London. Even when it was possible to distinguish the identity of the aircraft and to see the black crosses on the wings and tailplanes it was still hard to believe that this wasn't some peacetime exercise conducted by the Royal Air Force. Any doubts were soon dispelled when the first bombs hit the gasometers in Lewisham. Great gouts of orange flames and clouds of billowing black smoke filled the sky and soon fires were burning at New Cross, and at the Old Kent Road, where another set of gasometers was soon set ablaze. My train pulled into the station and I remember wondering whether we would make it home.

RAF Station Bassingbourn was a permanent establishment, having been built just before the war. It had four large hangars, permanent messes for officers, NCOS and airmen, as well as a large NAAFI canteen. The Station Commander was a Group Captain responsible for its administration as well as overseeing operations at two satellite airfields. One of these, near a sleepy village called Steeple Morden, was used by our instructors to give their students experience at landing on runways. These were laid out roughly in the form of an equilateral triangle providing six alternative directions of landing, according to wind speed and direction. Each flight took turns in providing maintenance personnel and groundcrews to support the daily flying operations, transport to and from the main field being provided by a three-ton Bedford lorry driven by airmen with varying degrees of driving skills and experience.

One damp spring morning in April, I was detailed for duty at Steeple Morden and was riding in the back of one of the shuttles, accompanied by half a dozen other 'erks' and a flying officer instructor from 'C' Flight who rode up front with the driver. Johnny and I were perched on the most desirable seat, on the tailgate, while the other airmen were resting against the slatted sides of the lorry, leaning their backs against the canvas canopy. On the floor in the centre was a large replacement glass lens and cover for the Chance light which was used for night-flying.

We were bumping along the narrow lane that led from the village to the airfield, enjoying the fresh smells of the countryside, when the driver swerved violently to the right, lost control, and rolled the Bedford into the ditch. The roll was almost in slow motion and no one was seriously hurt thanks to the grassy banks that lined the ditch. I landed with the back of my head resting against the soft canvas cover, while Johnny was thrown over to my side and cracked his head on the canopy frame. Miraculously, the precious Chance light lens somehow remained intact and we all crawled out on to the roadway making derogatory comments about the driver's lack of co-ordination. George, the driver, one of the airmen in our barrack room, came from Erdington, a suburb of Birmingham, and was, it appeared, destined to go through life as a loser. His head popped out of the cab and he shouted, "Fook me, ahve killt the officer," as he crawled through the window of the cab. "'Ere, gi' us some 'elp."

We scrambled up beside him and looked down into the cab, where the hapless officer was lying scrunched up in the corner.

"'Ave I killt 'im? 'E's not movin."

The officer opened one eye. "Of course I'm not movin', you clumsy clot, I've broken my bloody collar bone. Don't stand there gawking, get an ambulance."

Fortunately, the duty ambulance was only ten minutes behind us on its way to Steeple Morden and the officer's shoulder was soon strapped up and he was resting comfortably in Station Sick Quarters. Johnny and I thumbed a ride with an RASC vehicle that was on its way with the day's rations for the satellite. We were late for duty and feared the reception we might get from Flight Sergeant Fielding, but when he heard our story he was gruffly sympathetic and told us to get on with lighting the small stove in the cold, damp Nissen hut that served as a crew room for instructors and students.

The crew room was empty and Johnny went off to 'borrow' some kerosene from the bowser that carried fuel for the smoke pots used on night-flying operations. The sole fuel available for heating the Nissen huts was a very low grade of anthracite coke which would only burn with a good base of kindling and a strong draft. Lacking dry kindling, our technique was to crumple newspaper into tight balls and soak them in kerosene.

In order to increase the draft, we'd partly cover the grate with another sheet of newspaper and, after several attempts, and with liberal applications of kerosene from a corned beef can, a small glow could sometimes be achieved. On this day, we were frustrated in our attempts by damp paper, damp matches, and coke that refused to ignite, so we tossed the better part of a can of kerosene on the smoking mess. I threw in a lighted match, and we both leaned close to the grate and were blowing on the embers when the kerosene detonated with a loud explosion and a blast of soot that coated our faces and left us gasping and spluttering.

"Room, attention!" In strode Flight Sergeant Fielding, with brass shining and moustache bristling. "Stand to attention, officers present!"

Following him into the room were two very recognisable figures. The first, Marshal of the Royal Air Force Sir Hugh ('Boom') Trenchard, well over six feet in height, an impressive figure despite a slight stoop, leaned heavily on a cane. The second, unmistakably the country's leader, Prime Minister Winston Churchill, was clad in his usual boiler suit and with the inevitable cigar. The two of us stood rigidly to attention, hardly daring to breathe.

"And what are you two supposed to be doing?" asked Lord Trenchard.

Johnny was speechless, and I could only stammer, "Lighting a fire, sir."

The Prime Minister smiled, and took his cigar out of his mouth. "Why don't you try a little kerosene, my boy, that's what we used to use in the Boer War if we couldn't start a fire."

The two VIPs left the room chuckling, followed by Flight Sergeant Fielding, who paused just long enough to give us an ominous look.

"Report to me in the Orderly Room!" And with that he marched out and left us to contemplate our respective future careers in the Royal Air Force.

By the time we reported to Flight Sergeant Fielding, his wrath had subsided and he contented himself with tearing a strip off the three of us, concluding with a warning: "If I see any of you three back in this office you'll be confined to barracks."

It was my misfortune to be the next offender. Shortly after this event, I had frittered away an evening in the NAAFI canteen and had skipped cleaning my buttons before the Sunday morning church parade. The omission was missed by the inspecting officer, but didn't go unnoticed by the flight sergeant. He stopped in front of me and looked me up and down.

"You filthy airman. What's your name and number?"

"Robertson, 1383456, Flight Sergeant!"

"Right, you've lost it," he said, scribbling in his note book. "Report to the Orderly Room at 09:00 hours on Monday, you're on a charge."

The next morning, with battle dress pressed and boots shining, I waited outside the Orderly Room, with another offending sinner. It was George, our hapless driver of the squadron transport. He looked up at me, and moaned mournfully.

"Fook me, 'ow was I to know the cows were in t' road. Ah joost looked away for a second and ther' they were. What could ah do, 'it the fookin' cow?"

"Better than busting an officer's collar bone. I thought you were supposed to be getting married this weekend?"

"Ay, ah've put in for a forty-eight hour pass an' Flight said ah could 'ave it."

I couldn't help feeling sorry for poor George, although if truth were to be told much of his trouble came out of his environment. He'd grown up in the slums of Birmingham and I knew what a struggle he'd had to survive. But for my father's insistence that I accept a scholarship place at Wilson's Grammar School in Peckham, I wouldn't be any better off than George.

"Attention! Brinkley 338, right turn, quick march, left, right, left, right. Halt! Salute the officer." The Flight Sergeant shepherded George inside. The door into the Squadron Leader's office closed and I could only hear a low murmur of voices. Then the door opened and Brinkley was marched out.

"Robertson, 456! Right turn, quick march, left, right, left. Halt. Salute the officer." I stared straight ahead, saluted smartly and waited.

"Aircraftsman 1383456 Leonard Alan Robertson, you are charged under King's Regulations and Air Council Instructions with conduct prejudicial to good order and discipline in that you paraded for inspection at 10:00 hours on Sunday, April 12, 1941, and were found to be improperly dressed. Anything to say?"

"No, sir."

"Are you prepared to accept my summary punishment, or do you wish to be remanded to the Wing Commander Flying?"

"I'll accept your judgment, sir."

"Very well. I shall take into account that this is your first offence and award you seven days' confined to camp, with no loss of pay. But I want you to think about the consequences of your carelessness. An untidy turnout is a sign of an untidy mind. I see from your records that you are a Pilot U/T. Today

44

your actions are costing you no more than a little inconvenience. Tomorrow this kind of inattention to detail could cost you, and others dependent upon you, your lives. Don't let it happen again. Dismiss."

In a daze I saluted and marched out as the Flight Sergeant barked the time.

"Left, right, left! Halt, one-two! Now pay attention. Your punishment starts at 06:00 hours tomorrow, Tuesday, 13 April. Report to the Guard Room for inspection by the Orderly Officer. Number 1 Dress. Full marching order, with webbing clean and brasses shining. Same again at 18:00 hours. Is that clear?"

"Yes, Flight Sergeant."

"Report to your Flight, and try to keep out of trouble in future. Dismiss."

I hurried back through the hangar to 'C' Flight wondering how I was ever going to get ready for two daily inspections dressed in my best blues, clean all my equipment, and change back into working dress in time for work at 08:00 hours. When was I going to have time to line up at the Airmen's Mess for breakfast and dinner?

I hadn't counted on the camaraderie of the barracks. The twenty-four airmen who shared our barrack room came from all trades and had different lengths of service. Frank Wetherbie, one of the older men, had been an apprentice engine fitter at Halton before the war and served on the old aircraft carrier, Argus. His service number only had five digits (war-time recruits had seven!), and we all relied on his sage advice.

"Bit of bad luck getting nabbed by the Flight, young Robbie. But we'll all muck in and see you through. You look after your buttons and you can have my webbing belt tomorrow. My mate, Charlie, will lend you his rifle sling and Fred, here, will show you an old sweat's trick with your webbing gaiters.

"You'll see, your seven days' jankers will go in no time at all." He was right, of course. All the airmen united to enable a seemingly impossible task to be completed. Johnny and Farmer came back from the airmen's mess with my mug full of hot tea and a plate full of food "for our mate who is sick in the barrack room."

During the early days of the war, the Air Force was still small enough to have retained its peace time family atmosphere, and there was a distinct loyalty to the small units we lived in: barrack room, flight, squadron, command, or even the RAF itself. As with any family, the younger members were protected and instructed by their elders, who instilled in the next generation an unspoken pride of membership. In the same manner were traditions, myths, and legends passed on to new members of the family. This was reflected in the language and the vocabulary that we picked up in the barrack room at night as we were preparing our kit for the next day. A new recruit was referred to as a 'sprog,' and was told to 'get some service in.' 'Jankers' was punishment, 'Egyptian P.T.' was a euphemism for lying about and taking things easy. Many of these terms originated from the experience of old hands who had served overseas, like the Indian word 'charpoy' for bed, and the Arabic 'shufti' and 'dekko' for look.

Much of this lore was assimilated unconsciously, of course, and we picked up a lot more about life in the barracks after lights out. We were entertained by comedy dialogues performed with all the bawdy humour of the music hall comics of the 'thirties. Some wit would start with the cue line and the appropriate response would come from another part of the room:

(in a falsetto voice): "Dad, I want to go to the pictures."
(deeper and more gruffly): "Look at the pictures on the wall."
(falsetto): "But I want to see a moving picture."
(gruff): "I'll make the bugger move."
(falsetto): "Dad, I'm in the family way."
(gruff): "You're in every buggers way, get out of it."

(another gruff): "Into the woods!"

(falsetto): "I'll tell the vicar."

(gruff): "I am the vicar. Into the woods!"

(falsetto): "But I'm only thirteen."

(gruff): "This is no time for superstition. Into the woods!"

(falsetto): "Me mum's not goin' to like it."

(gruff): "Yer mum's not going to get it. Into the woods!"

This impromptu repartee would go on as long as half an hour without repetition until the corporal who slept in the corner bunk would call out: "Belt up. Time to get some kip." The response would be a loud fart then merciful silence. It all sounds pretty tame now, but for a seventeen-year-old boy from Brixton it was rather risqué. When I was growing up, my father would never swear or recount stories in bad taste. I remember when I was five, walking through our neighbourhood as we passed a local boy who was severely retarded. The kids used to run after him and chant, "Charlie, Charlie, stole some barley, out of the baker's shop." He would turn and curse them, as he did today when we came up behind him, "Fuck you, fuck you!" Dad simply took my hand and said, "Don't stare. He doesn't know any better. But you do. Don't ever let me hear you using such language." Dad was not well-educated, but he'd say, "No need to 'eff and blind'. Use language to express yourself properly."

George was a new phenomenon to me. I had grown up in a part of London that was largely populated by working class folk like my father. Dad had been discharged after the Great War with very little training and an education that ended when he was fourteen. Consequently, like thousands of others who were promised a land fit for heroes to live in, it was hard for him to find a job and a little too late to start apprenticing for a trade, as his father had done when he became a stonemason. Dad counted himself fortunate when he got a job as conductor on the double-decker trams, working from the tram depot at Camberwell Green. Most of the first twenty years of his service was spent on the Number 34 trams which ran from Chelsea to The Angel, Islington, via Clapham Common, Brixton, and Loughborough Junction, where we lived. Sometimes I would ride his tram home from school and I once saw him tell a cursing navvy to watch his tongue or he'd have to get off his tram. I suppose if I hadn't had his example I would have been just like George.

Fortunately for George, the Squadron Commander had dealt leniently with him, taking into account his short period of training and his inexperience as a motor transport driver, and had dismissed him with a caution. That meant he could go off on his forty-eight-hour pass and get married. As he told us all about it in the barrack room on his return, I couldn't help thinking of a cartoon character called Joe Bifstek, who went everywhere followed by a black cloud that poured hail, sleet, and snow all over him.

"Ah got away fro' 'ere on Friday after dooty. I 'itches a fookin' ride into Royston where I picks up a fookin' train for 'Itchen. 'Ow the fook was ah to know the next fookin' train to Crewe didn't leave 'til fookin' midnight? I kipped dahn on a fookin' bench in the waitin' room and fookin' near froze. Ah didn't get to Crewe until fookin six in t'mornin, and fookin' weddin's booked fer 'alf pas' fookin'one in th' afternoon. Mah train to Baremingum was 'eld up by fookin' troop trains an' ah didn't get 'ome 'til after one. Ah was in a right fookin' state, ah c'n tell yer. Got to church an' I din't know me fookin' arse from me elbow. Then we goes off t'pub for a pissup and we'd 'ardly had time for a fookin' pint when th' fookin' air-raid sirens went. Ah spent me 'ole fookin' weddin' night in fookin' pub cellar wi' fifty other people! Then ah 'ad ter leave fookin' 'ouse at seven ter get back 'ere by midnight. Joost mah fookin' look!"

The boys roared in merriment, more at the woeful look on George's face than at his misfortune. "Never mind, George," said Frank Weatherbie, "you'll be able to make an honest woman of her next leave."

Sadly, George never had a second chance because his new bride died in the rubble of her parents' house during an air-raid on the night after he got back to Bassingbourn. We sympathized with him and tried to cheer him up by taking him to the N.A.A.F.I. canteen for a few pints of mild and bitter. My abiding memory of George is of his crying softly into his beer.

Farmer, Johnny, and I found ourselves growing closer together while we were at Bassingbourn. Unlike Bridgenorth, where we were given very little spare time, we had regular duty hours with most evenings and weekends free to do as we wished. We were also treated as regular airmen and were frequently able to obtain weekend passes to visit our families. Farmer didn't find it worthwhile to try to make the trip to Shrewsbury unless he could get a seventy-two-hour pass, but John's parents lived at Watford, on the northern outskirts of London, and extended a generous invitation for us to stay with them whenever we had leave. It was fairly easy for us to hitch a ride, or we could catch a local train at Royston for Watford via Hitchin.

Johnny's mother was a wonderful cook, the three of us had big appetites, and we enjoyed many happy meals with the Kirby family. After dinner, Johnny's father would invite us down to the saloon bar of their local pub for a few beers, where we could have a relaxing game of darts, and where he could enjoy showing off his son and his son's new air force friends.

These carefree days were soon over when one morning we were summoned to the orderly room and told that the three of us had been posted to Cranwell in Lincolnshire. Cranwell was the home of the Royal Air Force College, and, as we happily packed our kitbags, we looked forward to starting our flying training with eager anticipation.

The bubble burst when we arrived at Cranwell and found that we were posted as aircraft hands, general duties. As we paraded in the motor pool yard with the other new arrivals, the Station Headquarters Flight Sergeant asked for three volunteers to step foward for special duties. Without hesitation, the three of us marched one pace forward. We found ourselves taking eight-hour shifts in the communications office, delivering teleprinter messages all over the station on our bicycle bearing the initials DRLS, which stood for 'Dispatch Rider Letter Service.' Not a mission of vital importance, but a small contribution to the war effort.

Since we worked on a shift system, we were excused all other duties and had the privilege of sleeping in our bunks when our barrack rooms were being inspected. I was awakened from a deep sleep one morning by Pete Spencer, who was acting room orderly. "Wake up. Come quick. Look at this. There's an aircraft taxiing without a propeller." I rushed outside the hut just in time to see Britain's first prototype jet fighter, the Gloster E28/39, later to be known as the Gloster Meteor. As we watched it carry out a high speed flypast, the thought crossed my mind that this new weapon could bring the war to an end before I had the chance to finish my training. In my naivete I didn't realise that it would take years to get from the test flight of prototype to the time that the production model would reach front line service. It was not until 1945 that the Meteor was supplied to Fighter Command in significant numbers and by then the war in Europe was nearly over.

It was during our short stay at Cranwell that we had our first taste of enemy action. As with most hostile encounters it was brief, exhilarating for a few moments, then over before we had time to be frightened. The cloudbase was at 700 feet and there was

about five-eighths of stratus, with another layer of complete cover at about 1,500 feet. A Heinkel 111 came flying over the camp between the cloud layers, must have caught a glimpse of the College buildings, and dropped a cluster of high explosive bombs. Only one of them dropped within the airfield boundary, landing in the Orange, a large expanse of grass lawn in front of the parade ground. The damage was  confined to a few broken windows and a small crater in the lawn. Much more exciting was the response of the Ground Defence Unit, roaring down the main road through camp in their Armadillo, an armoured half-ton lorry, firing off long bursts from their 40 mm. cannon with great panache, but with little or no effect. The last we saw of the Heinkel it was disappearing undamaged into the stratus cloud.

Such excitement paled into insignificance, however, when the next day we found our names in Station Standing Orders, promoting us to Leading Aircraftsmen and posting us to Number 3 Initial Training Wing at Torquay in Devon. At last our waiting was over and we were about to embark on the first stage of our training as pilots.

FOUR

In Search of Wings

I T WAS A HIGH-SPIRITED BAND of young men that boarded the bus at Cranwell. One over-zealous Daedalus managed to purloin the bus stop sign and was forever after known as 'Bus-stop Laggett.' Many of our companions would be at our side through the arduous twelve months ahead and we would get to know them through all their triumphs and reverses; but Farmer, Johnny, and I were never as close to the rest of them as we were to each other. Over a third were to fall by the wayside, some failing to meet the exacting standards set by the instructors, some losing their lives in training accidents.

Before we started our period of training at Torquay, we passed through an adjacent reception centre at Babbacombe. Instead of the standard barrack block we had been living in for the past six months, we were billeted in a requisitioned holiday hotel overlooking Babbacombe Beach. The three of us managed to wangle a room together and revelled in the privacy of our new accommodation. The purpose of the seven day stay at Babbacombe was to bring our clothing and equipment up to aircrew issue, and to fit us with flying gear. Naturally, we hurried back to our billets and tried everything on, gladly posing for Johnny, our amateur photographer, on the balcony. Never

mind that we sweltered in the semi-tropical heat of the Devonshire Riviera clad in Sidcot suit, helmet and goggles, sporting our
new canvas and leather-lined flying boots, and completing the
ensemble with new leather flying gauntlets over white silk
gloves. Looking back at those pictures now one might mistake us
for pilots of the Great War. Like us they flew in canvas-covered
biplanes and knew the rush of excitement as the slipstream from
the prop blasted our faces with the smells of engine oil and fresh
air. Flying conditions hadn't changed much since the time of the
Wright brothers.

At the end of the week we marched through the streets of
Torquay and arrived in the forecourt of another holiday hotel
that was to be our home for the next six weeks. The rumour
went around that 2,000 young women from the Prudential In-
surance Company had been evacuated to Torquay from London, and we weighed our chances of besporting ourselves on
the beaches with suntanned young maidens clad in skimpy
bathing costumes.

Our fantasies were destined to go unrealised as we were totally occupied with absorbing the incredible amount of learning that was to fill the next six weeks: aircraft recognition,
airmanship, more drill, elementary navigation and map reading, gunnery, morse code, theory of flight, unarmed combat,
and a gruelling commando training course that had us scaling
the local cliffs, and which culminated in a timed run over a
three mile obstacle course. After all this it was hardly any wonder that we had no energy left for the pursuit of more amorous
pleasures.

One highlight of the summer was my eighteenth birthday in
mid-June. Farmer and Johnny insisted that this auspicious occasion should be celebrated in style and invited me to drink as
many milk-shakes as I could consume. Wartime rationing
aside, the Devon milk bars produced a tasty blend of ice cream,
milk and syrups, and I managed to work my way steadily

through sixteen different flavours in under an hour. Johnny suggested that a stroll into Cockington might help my digestion and I dutifully agreed, walking between them as eight pints of fluid sloshed around in my belly. I think I might have been all right had not Johnny persuaded me that a pint of rough cider at the Old Forge Inn might suitably cap the celebration. As I sat in the hot sun in the pub garden trying to get a pint of cider down into an already distended stomach, a synapse closed somewhere in my central nervous system and my brain got the message. I just made it to the gents' in time and returned to my two companions paler and lighter. Such are the recuperative powers of the young that we were all three sitting down to an enormous supper of fish and chips within an hour.

In addition to a final week of exams, we were subjected to a barrage of psychological tests to determine our suitability for one of the three operational commands: fighter, bomber or coastal, or our aptitude as instructors in Training Command. Of course, we were not given the results of these diagnostic tests, but they were in large measure to determine what sort of aircraft we flew on completion of our flying training.

SIX

Sic Transit

BY THE END OF JUNE 1941 we had finished our course in the Initial Training Wing (ITW) and were sent on seven days' embarkation leave, indicating to us that we were to be part of the Commonwealth Training Plan and destined for flying training overseas in Canada, Rhodesia or South Africa. At the end of our leave we reported to Wilmslow, an RAF Reception Centre near Manchester, to await the next available troopship. Our draft consisted of ninety-three cadet pilots drawn from all parts of the British Isles housed in a drill hall furnished with double-tier bunks and crammed together in a space normally occupied by twenty-four airmen. We were issued with tropical drill shirts and slacks, as well as a mysterious item of apparel in the form of a grey flannel suit from Burton's, the Fifty Shilling Tailors. There was much speculation over the latter, but our curiosity was not answered until later.

At the end of the week we boarded a small Irish ferry boat and set sail for Iceland. The short voyage was rough and Farmer and Johnny spent much of the time on deck, miserable and seasick. Perhaps because of my resilient digestive system I managed to eat most of the meals and to keep them down. Everyone was relieved when we landed at Reykjavik and found ourselves in a small transit camp near Thingfallir Hot Springs. The Camp Commandant was a Wing Commander who had been recalled from retirement and was a bit of an anachronism in that he appeared on parade for our weekly inspection wearing riding breeches and boots that had become obsolete well before the war. He was harmless enough but quite batty. We had some trouble getting used to the long hours of daylight and found it difficult to sleep on the floor of our unheated Nissen hut. We had no duties or responsibilities and occupied ourselves by riding the shaggy Icelandic ponies and swimming at the local sulphur hot springs, especially when we discovered that the distant but beautiful Icelandic women wore no bathing suits. Tensions were relieved when an east-bound convoy arrived from Halifax carrying a draft of RCAF aircrews bound for England, and we gladly took their places on the Ascania, a converted passenger liner of the White Star Line, now serving as what the Royal Navy euphemistically had classified as an armed merchant cruiser.

Because of its six-inch guns, the Ascania made the west bound trip to Halifax unescorted, clipping along at fifteen knots and zigzagging to provide a difficult target for U-boats. Our small draft of ninety-three men was assigned to 'F' Deck, or the glory hole as it was referred to by the merchant navy crew. We were issued with mattresses and Farmer, Johnny, and I claimed adjacent places against the bulkhead of an open space which served as the ship's cinema. We were not allowed on deck after dark and were able to watch movies while lying in our beds. Unfortunately, the ship carried only one film, "The Four Feathers," with John Clements and Ralph Richardson, so we were forced to see the same program eleven nights in a row. By the end of the voyage each of us could play any one of the roles. My favourite scene was the one in which a sunblinded Richardson returns to his camp only to find his whole unit wiped out by the Fuzzy Wuzzies. He staggers blindly between the tents assailed by the raucous cries of the scavenging vultures, and is saved by Clements, who has been dubbed a coward by his fellow officers for resigning his commission on the eve of the regiment's departure for the Sudan. It was probably intended to be a serious comment on the inhumanity of war, but we saw it as a hilarious comedy.

The only other excitement we had at sea was when we were approaching Newfoundland and the Captain decided to give his gunnery crews some practice by firing a salvo from his six-inch guns. It was a deafening sound and as the hull shuddered we couldn't help wondering if the whole ship might not split asunder and plunge us all to the bottom of the Atlantic. Fortunately we made it to Halifax unscathed by enemy U-boats or friendly fire. After disembarking at Halifax we were paraded and given a week's pay and six hours of shore leave. We made our way downtown, enjoyed our first North American meal, apple pie and ice-cream at the YMCA, and went to our first movie in Canada. I recall coming out of the dark into the bright lights of the main thoroughfare and contrasting them with the nightly blackout we'd left behind us in England.

We boarded a Canadian National Railway troop train and wound our way slowly via Montreal to Toronto, where we were billeted in the Canadian National Exhibition buildings. We found ourselves occupying the bull ring in the Agricultural Hall and from the smell it was evident that the former occupants had only recently left.

The hall was a vast sea of double-tier bunks and we had little to do for the next ten days but to attend lectures on personal hygiene illustrated with horrifyingly explicit details of the consequences of exposure to venereal disease, accompanied by the exhortation not to pass by the guard house without picking up a prophylactic.

The next day was a Sunday and Toronto lived up to its reputation as a joyless city on the sabbath. The three of us were standing on the corner of Yonge and Bloor when we were hailed by a rotund little man with horn-rimmed spectacles, the very epitome of an American businessman.

"Hi, fellas. You from the old country? Thornton's the name. Al Thornton. Say, how would you guys like to come to dinner with me tonight? Just tell me where and I'll pick you up at six."

We were not used to receiving such generous invitations from complete strangers, but we accepted with alacrity. It looked like being a dull Sunday and the food at the Manning Depot, while adequate and nutritious for our needs, lacked something in aesthetic pleasure, served as it was in a dining hall that seated 1,000 ravenous airmen. The prospect of a free restaurant meal was not to be refused lightly, but nothing could have prepared us for the elegance of the old Granite Club. Our host picked us up at six, as promised, and drove us to the club in his magnificent Packard Clipper convertible. We were seated by a deferential waiter who obviously knew Mr. Thornton as a long time member and a generous tipper.

I had not seen such an array of silver and table settings and followed Johnny's lead in the choice of utensils for each course. We had soup, salad, fish, an entree, and a dessert, each course accompanied by an appropriate wine, culminating in a fine old Napolean brandy and a Cuban cigar. All the while our host enquired of our homes and families, asked us for our impressions of Canada, and told us a little about his business and his family.

"Say, how long are you guys here? Sure would like you to see something of our country outside of Toronto. Could you get leave next weekend? I'd like you to meet my family, have dinner with us on Saturday, and maybe we could drive down to Niagara through the peach district."

We were completely charmed by this man and overwhelmed by his generosity. We gladly accepted his invitation and arranged to meet him at the gates of the exhibition grounds at one o'clock on Saturday afternoon.

He proudly introduced us to his wife, his daughter, and a son, Tom, who seemed to be about our age, and who was a student at the University of Toronto. The whole family treated us as honoured guests in their home, a foretaste of the warmth and generous hospitality that we were to experience during our entire stay in North America.

Mrs. Thornton was an excellent cook and kept our plates filled until we reluctantly protested that we simply couldn't eat another bite or drink another drop. At the end of a delightful evening of good food and stimulating conversation we retired to our comfortable bedrooms. Next morning, after a hearty breakfast, we were on the road to the Niagara Peninsula, Johnny sitting up front with Tom and his dad, while Farmer and I shared the rumble seat.

It was a glorious July day and the air was warm and fragrant with the smells of the countryside. Tom stopped the car at a wayside fruit stand and Mr. Thornton bought a couple of baskets of ripe peaches for sixty cents. Farmer and I had a great time with each mouthful of luscious fruit and I couldn't help remembering that the last time I had seen a fresh peach it was on solitary display in a Piccadily fruit shop. One peach cost seven shillings and six pence, about two dollars, and here we were eating peaches that cost about five cents each. It reminded us how lucky we were to have been granted even a brief respite from wartime England with its rationing.

When we got back to barracks after our wonderful weekend with the Thorntons, we found our movement order posted on the bulletin board.

We were to parade at 07:00 hours the following day and board buses for Union Station where we were to entrain for Detroit via Windsor. And we were ordered to dress in those mysterious grey suits. Garbed in look-alike outfits, we must have looked like refugee spivs from Portobello Road.

After a short ferry ride across the Detroit River, we were loaded into U.S. Navy buses and, complete with police motorcycle escort, we wailed our way to the U.S. Navy Elimination Base at Grosse Ile, Michigan, an ominous name and one that was to fulfil its stated purpose of weeding out those who had no aptitude for flying.

An RAF Liaison Officer was on hand to greet us and to brief us on the reason for our civilian dress and to settle the mystery of those grey suits. In August 1941, the United States was technically a non-belligerent power and as such was expected to behave as a neutral nation. We were part of the Lend-Lease deal that the British and American governments had signed. We were to be trained side by side with American Flight Cadets and were to be accorded no special treatment. We would wear U.S. Navy khaki drill uniforms, but would retain our RAF headgear. Off base we would wear our grey flannel suits and behave like civilians. In fact, we were issued with a small blue book compiled by the British government laying out a code of behaviour for us to follow. It started off by saying that just because we spoke the same language we should not always expect to understand Americans, and vice versa. It contained a glossary of terms that prepared us for some of the language and idiomatic differences, but it hardly prepared us for every occasion. One of our number was approached at the depot by a sweet young thing who asked him, "Do you shag?" His embarrassment was somewhat mollified when he discovered that she was merely trying to ascertain whether he liked to dance.

We learned that we were to be at Grosse Ile for only three weeks, in which time we would be required to attend lectures and to go solo on the elementary training aircraft known as an N3N-3, a two-seater biplane built at the Naval Aircraft Factory in Philadelphia. It was a rugged little machine and was designed to absorb an enormous amount of punishment.

My instructor was Lieutenant William Dietrich, a tall, taciturn

U.S. Marine. He hardly said more than a few words to me in the four and a half hours of dual instruction he gave me. It was somewhat of a shock, therefore, when he got out of the aircraft after a bumpy landing I had just executed and nodded briefly.

"You're ready," he said. "Just carry out one circuit and landing and I'll see you in the Ready Room."

I sat for a moment, stunned. How could I be ready for solo? I hadn't had the minimum of five hours' instruction yet. As I sat there in a daze one of the U.S. Navy ground crew came out and tied a small red drogue to the intersection strut on either wing, a sign to other aircraft that a first solo flight was being made.

I waved to the mechanic and taxied to the down wind end of the field, turned cross wind, checked for other traffic on the approach, locked the tail wheel and opened the throttle to full power. As the aircraft gathered speed I eased the stick forward and the tail came up. Countering the torque action of the prop I held on a little right rudder and kept the aircraft's nose pointing into wind. Almost without my hand willing it the wheels left the ground and the little biplane climbed smoothly into the clear blue sky. At 500 feet I started a rate one turn on to the downwind leg and reduced power as the altimeter reached 1,000 feet. I looked at the leading edge of the port wing and as the landing point disappeared from view I throttled back completely and started a gentle gliding turn on to the final approach. As I crossed the boundary of the field, I eased the stick back and felt all three wheels touch the ground at the same time. There was no bounce and I managed to keep the aircraft running straight ahead to the circular taxiway that ran all round the field. I had successfully finished my first solo flight! The aircraft came to a rumbling stop and I gave the engine a burst of power and applied full rudder and brake to turn left in the direction of the flight line. Nothing happened. I increased the power a little and braked harder. No turn. I throttled back and sat there perplexed until a crewman came out and unlocked the tailwheel!

I walked from the flight line into the hangar believing that all my fellow cadets were waiting to tease me about forgetting to unlock the tailwheel, and it was with embarrassment that I reported to my instructor in the Ready Room.

"That was just about the best damned landing I've seen in a long time," he said. "I'd say that that deserves a special kind of award, don't you, fellas?"

He grinned at my classmates and gave them a wink. Before I knew it I was hoisted shoulder high and carried down to the seaplane dock, where I was unceremoniously tossed into the cool waters of the Detroit River, apparently the customary accolade reserved for the first cadet in each class to fly solo.

Before we left Grosse Ile, we were invited by Henry Ford Jr. to visit the big assembly plant just outside Detroit where the new scout car, later to be known as the Jeep, was being mass produced for the U.S. Department of Defence. We were all wearing our grey flannel suits, including the RAF Liaison Officer, and we posed for a group photograph in front of the Jeep.

Two of our number, brasher than the rest, asked if they could take the Jeep for a lap around the test track. Mr. Ford graciously assented and the Jeep took off like a startled jackrabbit. The driver's experience was limited to driving nothing more powerful than an Austin Seven and he was unprepared for the

torque and acceleration of the little scout car. He hit a mound in the middle of the track doing about forty miles an hour and the Jeep became airborne.

When it came to rest the Jeep had a broken front axle, the driver had a broken wrist, and his passenger had lost two front teeth. Our visit came to an abrupt end and we were ushered back into our buses and returned to base. We had been promised a slapup dinner in the Rotunda, but we gathered that Anglo-American friendship had failed to stand up to the test, as had the Jeep at the hands of our two classmates.

SEVEN

Through These Portals

W E KNEW AS SOON AS WE ARRIVED at the United States Naval Air Station, Pensacola, Florida, that we were at the Annapolis of the Air. Everything, from the smartly turned out U.S. Marine guard at the main gate, to the neatly laid out and carefully groomed roads and gardens of the base, the purposeful squads of flight cadets marching to classes, the white painted barrack blocks, all spoke of the character of the place. Here, people knew what they were about; they set high standards for themselves and had high expectations of others. We recognised that this peacetime training base was dedicated to producing career officers equivalent to those young men who were at similar institutions in Britain: the Royal Military College at Sandhurst, the Royal Naval College at Dartmouth, and the Royal Air Force College at Cranwell.

We plunged straight away into the rigorous training program with a two-week period of indoctrination. Our days started early, with reveille at 05:30 hours, calisthenics at 06:00, and breakfast at 06:30 in the Commissary. A number of tables were assigned to the British Flight Cadet Battalion and we dined like the American flight cadets. Not only were we treated like officer cadets and served by mess orderlies in crisp white uniforms, we also enjoyed the best of meals in a seemingly un-ending quantity. One had only to ask and eggs would be cooked to order. There was an endless supply of fresh coffee and fruit juices. The only constraint was time.

Our barrack rooms, or 'decks' as they were referred to by our officers, had to be ready for inspection before we left for the day's classes. Bunks had to be made in a precise way so that the top blanket was turned down exactly six inches and drawn so tautly that the inspecting officer could bounce an American quarter coin on it. We soon learned that any slackness or inatten-tion to detail could earn up to three or five demerit points. A to-tal of twelve points could result in suspension from flying training, and for the offender, could mean being returned to Britain and consequently being dropped from aircrew training.

Needless to say the system provided a strong incentive to toe the line, but it also created some resentment, particularly among the more experienced men, many of whom had already seen action and wanted to get back into the war.

One of these was Tiny Batt, who had been a sergeant in a guards regiment at the retreat from Dunkirk. He was accustomed to the spit and polish life of a front line regiment, but for him many of the petty restrictions were childish and irksome. How-ever, he was mature enough to recognise that the main purpose of our being here was to get the training that would turn us into ef-fective and efficient aircrew, and he kept his feelings in check. He was a good example to the rest and eventually became an under-officer in charge of the British Flight Cadet Battalion.

The other cause of irritation was the indoctrination part of the course. We knew that it was primarily intended for the Ameri-can cadets, who had just finished high school or the first year of college, and who had no idea of the routines of military life. Still, it was rather tedious to go through much of what we had al-ready been taught at recruit training and Initial Training Wing, including customs of the service like saluting and military drill, particularly when we thought that U.S. Navy marching drill was sloppy and inferior to ours.

I think the final test of our patience came when we were divided into crews to man ship's boats called cutters, and were tongue-lashed by young ensigns who exhorted us to greater efforts than we were prepared to exert. Tiny Batt summed it up for all of us when he remarked that he didn't intend to row his way into battle, but his way of showing his contempt for the whole process was to stroke his crew into winning the pennant for the best team effort.

Another problem we faced was our syllabus of training showing that it would be nearly three months before we began flying, and were required to complete a ground course syllabus which repeated much of our basic training at I.T.W. including morse, semaphore, and aircraft recognition. Some of the new material, however, was interesting and challenging, and was to prove particularly useful later when we became captains of our own aircraft. We learned the intricate functioning of the Stromberg injection carburetor and spent many hours at the engine test beds discovering how to troubleshoot the Pratt & Whitney Twin Wasp power plants.

With the beginning of ground school we were extended the privilege of week- end leave provided that we returned to base by 21:20 hours in time for lights out. Our concept of the deep south was inspired by movies we had seen back home. "Gone With the Wind" had been released in England just before the outbreak of war and I am sure that it coloured our vision of our stay in Pensacola. The city itself was full of history, but it was the prospect of meeting a Southern Belle that excited many young British flight cadets, and if we found their southern drawl to be appealing they were no less impressed by our clipped English accents. If we were looking for a Vivien Leigh or a Claudette Colbert, they were expecting every young Englishman to be a Leslie Howard or a David Niven.

Farmer, Johnny, and I visited the First Methodist Church in Pensacola one Sunday in September. Farmer attended a Congregational Church in Shrewsbury and I had just been confirmed in the Church of England before we had left Torquay. Johnny did not attend church regularly but liked to shop around.

We were standing outside the church after the service when a gracious lady and her husband asked us home to lunch with them. We were introduced to their children, Jane, who was twenty-one, Emma a shy sixteen, and Rob, the youngest, who was fourteen. Mr. and Mrs. Palmer lived in a modest home in North Spring Street; he was an industrial chemist, she a published author. Their comfortable house was to become our home away from home for the better part of a year. Their friends became our friends as we were drawn into their social circle and we were invited to join in their family celebrations at Thanksgiving, Christmas, and the New Year. Johnny and I, in our turn, invited the daughters to the formal dances that were held at the San Carlos Hotel on Palafox Street.

Johnny dated Jane quite regularly, and I was generally in company with Emma and her best friends: Boo, Anne, Leatha Mae, and Joyce. They were all juniors at Pensacola High School, and much more sophisticated than I, having had the benefit of a co-educational education system, whereas I had attended a school for boys only. I must have seemed awkward and gauche to them, but they were generous and forgiving. I learned to relax with them, eventually outgrew my shyness in their company and, with Emma's encouragement, even made my first faltering efforts to dance.

Meanwhile, ground school had finally come to an end and we were assigned to our basic training squadrons. Johnny, Farmer, and I were to be flying out of Saufley Field, about half an hour's bus ride from the main Pensacola airbase.

We had to be on the flight line for the first detail at 07:00 and those early morning rides in an open bus were designed to keep us awake and alert.

There were four phases to our flying instruction: basic, advanced, instrument, and flying boat training. Each stage introduced more sophisticated aircraft and demanded of us increasing degrees of accuracy in flying and higher standards of airmanship.

It became evident on our first day at Saufley Field that the basic squadron was going to be no piece of cake. I was assigned a navy instructor named Ensign Garber who spent some time briefing me on the syllabus. Even though I had soloed on the aircraft we would be flying, the N3N-3 biplane, I would still have to satisfy my instructor that I was fit to fly solo. I discovered that there was a greater stress on accuracy here and that approximate heights and speeds were not acceptable. If Ensign Garber wanted me to fly at 3,000 feet, and at eighty knots, that's what he meant. 3,100 feet or eighty-five knots was not good enough.

At regular intervals in the course we were required to pass a check flight with another instructor. If he was not satisfied that we were ready for the next stage and gave a thumbs down we were checked again by a third instructor. If he gave a thumbs down, we were booked to ride with the squadron commander and if he was not satisfied we flunked the course and were returned to Canada. There was no appeal and no further possibility of pilot training with the RAF. We lived constantly with the knowledge that high standards were required and that there was no excuse for failure.

I slid by the 'A' and 'B' check flights successfully, but had some trouble with the 'C' check, which not only required precision aerobatics, but also a forced landing procedure which involved making a glide landing from 1,000 feet and a three-point touchdown within a fifty foot white circle marked on the grass field, a minimum of five out of six attempts. I excelled at aerobatics and made it a point to line up the aircraft's nose on a prominent highway and fly my wing over turns exactly 180 degrees to each other. However, when it came to hitting the circle for the forced landing procedure I missed the first and sixth attempts. The instructor gave me a thumbs down and I went to meet Ensign Garber with a heavy heart.

"Don't let it get to you," he said. "I'll schedule you with another instructor right away, and I know you'll make it. Just take it easy and don't get flustered."

With the second instructor everything went smoothly and I scored six out of six circle shots. Then, in the afternoon, the third instructor gave me a thumbs up with five out of five and a close miss on the sixth shot. With great relief I boarded the bus back to the main base.

I knew as soon as I saw Johnny that something was wrong. He looked as though he'd been put through a wringer and hung out to dry. He made all the circle shots but as soon as he got to the aerobatic sequences he became violently airsick and had to abandon the check flight. A second check flight was arranged for the next day, but Johnny had lost all confidence.

"It's not going to get any better," he shrugged. "I might as well face it that I'm never going to be a pilot. The best I can hope for is a navigator's course in Canada. Who knows, I might get lucky and finish my course before you two."

Much as we tried to boost Johnny's confidence, Farmer and I could not shake him from the inevitable outcome of tomorrow's check flight. And in the end it turned out the way Johnny had predicted. The one-third attrition rate took its toll of our trio and we were to become a twosome. We said farewell to Johnny at the end of January and life went on.

Farmer and I passed our 'D' and 'E' checks and moved on to advanced flying. The advanced flying squadron was equipped with Vought Sikorsky OS2U-3s and Vultee Valiants. The first was the carrier version of a single-float fleet scouting aircraft. It

was equipped with a fixed undercarriage, but had hydrauli-
cally operated flaps and wheel brakes. It was heavy to handle,
particularly at landing speed, and lateral control become rather
sluggish. This characteristic coupled with a rather narrow
wheel track combined to make it prone to ground loop if the
wing was allowed to drop just before touchdown.

Compared with the old N3N-3 it was quite a handful, but it
was nothing to the handling required of the Vultee Valiant. It
had a retractable undercarriage, wing flaps, and our first taste
of radio voice communication in the shape of a four channel
Very High Frequency Radio. Juggling all these new controls as
well as flying this sleek, high performance all-metal monoplane was quite a challenge. Small wonder that we called it the
Vultee 'Vibrator,' though it was our jangled nerves that did the
vibrating!

One of the important aspects of advanced flying was formation practice. This involved our forming up in four sections of
three aircraft in a diamond box formation. The lead aircraft carried an instructor and a student, but the remaining eleven were
piloted by solo students. To add interest to the exercise the
whole formation was monitored by an instructor in a thirteenth
plane who was known as the chase pilot. He kept up a constant
stream of patter to coax the laggards to close up and whenever
a student was slow to respond he would literally snap at his
heels like a sheepdog.

One of our British pilots fell victim to an over-zealous chase
pilot who buzzed him too closely and sheared off his tailplane
with his propeller. As a result Flight Cadet Tipple from Ontario
had to bail out and narrowly escaped injury when his parachute opened just as he entered a flowering apple tree. His
nickname of 'Blossom' stayed with him from that day on.

Two other student pilots were not so lucky when their aircraft got too close and the resulting collision prevented them

from making an emergency descent by parachute. Their bodies were recovered from the cockpits of their aircraft still securely fastened by their harnesses. The RAF Liaison Officer had the sad duty of clearing their lockers and of sending their personal effects to their next of kin with an accompanying letter of condolence.

I would not like to give the impression that we were unaffected by these losses, or that we were unduly preoccupied with thoughts of flying accidents and their inevitable consequences. I am sure that the natural resilience of youth helped us to find ways of coping with the simple fact that we were not all going to survive the hazards of flying training.

There were many outlets for us to rid ourselves of the daily tensions of life, including sports, of course, and we readily adapted to the North American games of baseball and football. What we never could get accustomed to was the way the spectators would keep up a running barrage of advice, criticism, and invective. Our responses tended to follow the customs of our national games of soccer and cricket, so it was a little incongruous for the American flight cadets to hear an occasional comment like "Well done, nice hit!" or "Well tackled!"

We also found time to publish a student newspaper called 'Limey.' Looking through editions of this publication over sixty years later is a reminder of the way we were able to take a professional attitude to our work without taking ourselves too seriously. Much of the humour is directed towards our own follies. There is, for instance, a wonderful series of cartoons called 'He trained at Pensacola,' which showed how our new-found habits and customs might be received on our return to Britain. They were contributed by a British Flight Student, the son of a well-known British illustrator, Trevor Evans, who made a gift of one of his own creations to celebrate our first Christmas issue in December 1941.

XMA/ GRELTING/ TO THE BOY/ OF THE R.F.B.

The next phase of our training lasted only three weeks, but what it lacked in duration it more than made up for in its concentration and intensity. By now we had amassed a total of 300 flying hours and were considered to be competent to fly an aluminium-clad 'whirling bucket of bolts' propelled by a 750 horse-power radial engine, and equipped with the latest refinements in military aviation design, including retractable landing gear, hydraulic brakes and flaps and a sophisticated VHF radio system. We flew by day only, and under visual flight rules, which meant that we were only fair weather pilots.

Number Three Squadron operated out of Chevalier Field, which was on the main base and within walking distance of our barracks. Thus we were spared the early morning ride in a draughty semi-articulated trailer and could devote our whole day and energies to the rigours of all-weather flying. At the end of this stage of our flying training lay the coveted prize of a blind flying ticket, together with the endorsement of being 'qualified to let down on instruments.'

As with our basic and advanced stages of instruction the emphasis was on exact and precise flying within extremely narrow tolerances. Before we were allowed to climb into the cockpit of the SNJ-3, or North American Harvard, we had to master the intricate procedures of the radio range on a flight simulator called the Link Trainer. Dozens of these simulators were housed in classrooms built on to the sides of the hangars that accommodated the Harvards on which we were to hone our instrument-flying skills.

The instructors operating the Link Trainers were civilian men and women but were every bit as demanding as our Navy flying instructors who worked together with their civilian counterparts to monitor the progress of every student. The results of each simulated flight were recorded on a chart that showed the configuration of the particular radio range station in the local flying area, in our case the range at Foley, Alabama.

A device called a 'crab' traced the path of the aircraft with an inked stylus so that the instructors could assess the student's capabilities in identifying, bracketing, and homing in on the beam. The student pilot's ear phones conveyed the sounds which would enable him to simulate a blind approach. Four beams emanated from the transmitter and flying along the centre of the beam produced a steady note that grew or faded in volume depending on whether you were approaching or leaving the airfield. Flying to one side or the other of the beam produced an 'A' or an 'N' signal in morse (dit-dah or dah-dit), depending on which of the four quadrants the aircraft was flying.

In addition to the task of interpreting his geographical position, the pilot had to maintain control of the aircraft's attitude in three planes: pitching, yawing, and rolling. This meant an intense visual concentration on the flight instruments that gave these items of information: artificial horizon, vertical speed indicator, airspeed indicator, altimeter, turn and bank indicator, gyro compass, and magnetic compass. While the student pilot attempted to co-ordinate both visual and aural sources of information, the instructor could make things even more difficult by simulating turbulence or rough air.

Daytime temperatures in Florida were in the high eighties, there was no air-conditioning in the hangars, and the sustained concentration over an hour- and-a-half period turned the simulator exercises into a form of excruciating torture and usually resulted in the luckless victim being saturated in sweat and suffering from a splitting headache. It was, therefore, with great relief that we moved on to put the lessons learned on the simulator into practical use in the air.

I always looked forward to the first flight of the day, when the air was cool and stable. The instructor would be in the front seat with the student seated behind and beneath a canvas canopy that excluded all view of the outside. At first the instructor would carry out the take-off and the student would follow through on the controls, but after a certain amount of practice the roles would be reversed and the student would carry out a blind take-off with the instructor following him through on the controls. Once in the air, the radio would be tuned to the range station and the student would carry out an orientation exercise and make an actual blind approach and landing. The satisfaction of making a letdown on instruments, controlling the aircraft and making all the necessary cockpit checks, was reward enough for all the tiresome hours spent in the simulator.

After I had completed the letdown exercise my instructor would challenge my skills even further by putting the aircraft into an unusual position and handing over control to me with the artificial horizon and gyro compass toppled and spinning madly, leaving me to recover control using only airspeed indicator, altimeter, and turn and bank indicator. I loved the challenge and developed an ability to return the aircraft to level flight with the minimum loss of height. In later years, flying in all weathers over the Atlantic in winter, or over the Indian

Ocean in the monsoons, I was to be grateful for the training I'd received in Squadron Three. The Chief Flight Instructor, Captain Lanman, of the United States Marines, gave me a final piece of advice after the check flight that earned me my instrument rating: "Keep practising! You'll never regret the hours you spend 'under the hood.' One day those skills will get you out of a sticky situation, and may mean the difference between life and death for you and your crew."

The following Monday I reported to the Big Boat Hangar, Squadron Four.

As I looked up at the enormous bulk of the P2Y-2 towering above me on the hard standing I felt at last the thrill of graduating to an operational aircraft. The P2Y-2 was a twin-engined biplane flying boat with its Twin Wasp power plants mounted between the two main planes. The hull was sheathed with a thin duraluminium plating, but its wings and tail plane were fabric-covered. The pilots' cockpit was enclosed and roomy and was connected to the main cabin by a watertight bulkhead. The main cabin housed the navigator, radioman, and an ordnance man who was responsible for all the armaments: depth charges, bombs, machine guns, and signal flares.

The P2Y-2 was designed and built by the Consolidated Aircraft Company in San Diego, California, and had been the workhorse of the U.S. Fleet as a patrol bomber and general reconnaissance aircraft since the early 1930s. By 1942 it had be-

come obsolete as a fighting aircraft and had been relegated to the role of training flying boat crews, but for us it meant the application of all we had learned in our flying training to date. By this time I had amassed some fifty hours dual and 100 hours solo flying, not a large sum, but infinitely greater than the pilots who fought in the Great War, who often went into action with as little as twelve hours in total flying experience.

Farmer and I, together with three other British Flight Cadets, were assigned to Ensign Jennings, who gave us our first familiarisation flight in the P2Y-2. I was first in the lefthand seat, with the instructor in the copilot's position and the other four looking over our shoulders. Looking from the cockpit down on to the concrete apron, it seemed that we were thirty feet off the ground, an illusion caused in part because the aircraft was resting on landing gear that would be retrieved by the beaching crew after we had rolled down the ramp into the waters of Escambia Bay. Instead of a single control column there was a heavy yoke which carried two wheels that controlled the ailerons and moved the aircraft in the rolling plane. Pushing the yoke in the fore and aft plane actuated the elevators and caused the nose to pitch up or down. In addition, each pilot could control the twin rudders by means of foot pedals.

As the instructor advanced both throttles we could feel the power behind the twin Hamilton variable pitch propellers, and the big boat slowly moved toward the ramp on its beaching gear. As we crested the slope he throttled back to an idle and allowed the weight of the aircraft to carry us down to the water. The beaching crew, dressed in buoyancy suits and up to their necks in water, quickly released the retaining pins and the beaching wheels were pulled clear of the hull, leaving the twenty-ton boat rocking gently in the water and tied to land only by a stern line.

Once Ensign Jennings was sure that the beaching gear had been released and that the beaching crew were clear, he signalled for the stern line to be dropped and taxied out into the alighting area. After a brief take-off check, he swung the aircraft into wind and steadily moved the throttles to the fully open position and at the same time hauled the yoke back into his chest. Within a very short run the hull was riding up on to the step and he was able to ease the yoke forward until the hull was barely skimming the water. Then, as the airspeed built up to fifty-five knots, he moved the elevator trim wheel slightly aft and the flying boat left the water and rose majestically into the air. As he trimmed forward to gain flying speed, climbing slowly into the blue sky of the Gulf of Mexico, I had the feeling that this is what I was always intended to be: part aviator and part mariner, sometimes waterborne, sometimes airborne, operating in the elements of sea and air that required a fine admixture of the skills of airmanship and seamanship.

Ensign Jennings pointed out a large red and white marker buoy that was just passing under the port wing and gently throttled back until the big motors were whispering quietly and starting a gentle turn into the wind whose direction was indicated by windlanes caused by the wave tops breaking and forming streaks of foam. As we neared the surface he gently eased back on the yoke and the tip of the keel touched lightly and the patter of water striking the hull rose to a crescendo of sound. The boat alighted with the grace of a swan and, as the speed dropped off, the hull sank lower and lower until we were riding gently on the water with our two propellers idling and the tailplane and rudders keeping us facing into the wind.

"One circuit and landing each, and then we break for lunch. You have control, Robertson." Ensign Jennings opened his side window and rested his arm on the sill as though his responsibilty was over.

I carried out the pre-take-off check, swung the aircraft into wind and set the gyro compass. Heaving back on the wheel with one hand, I advanced the throttles to the take-off setting, and kept the wings level with the horizon as the nose rose and the hull lifted up onto the step. It was incredible how much sheer muscular heft it required to keep the yoke back into one's chest, and, just when I thought my biceps would yield, the nose eased forward and we were skimming over the surface with the airspeed indicator showing that it was time to part company with the waves.

A gentle backward pressure of the wheel and we were airborne. I grinned over my shoulder to Farmer and set the throttles to climbing power and the pitch control to 2,400 RPM. All too soon the marker buoy slid under the wing and I began the landing check as I turned into wind for my first touchdown on water. I found that the aircraft trimmed well and responded to the lightest touch on the controls, so that when it came time to flare out it required but a tiny backward movement of the yoke to bring the huge aircraft into the landing attitude. A gentle kiss of the water on the hull and we were slowing down to taxiing speed. It was all over in three minutes. I had pulled off my first take-off and landing on water and was incurably in love with flying boats.

Ensign Jennings raised his thumb and I changed places with Farmer, who settled into my seat while I moved aft to watch his performance from the main cabin. Steady as a rock, Farmer flew the circuit like a pro and touched down right beside the marker buoy. He completed the necessary check and handed over control to the instructor. The other three quickly followed suit and all too soon it was time for lunch. Instead of our returning to the landing ramp, the ordnance man handed out a sandwich lunch, consisting of chocolate milk and peanut butter sandwiches, and we ate as we sat bobbing on the sunlit waters of the bay with our motors switched off and the water lapping gently on the side of the hull. It was the life of a flying boat skipper for me from then on!

What followed was weeks of joyous freedom as we practised various kinds of landings: glide, power-assisted, and fully-stalled or rough sea landings. Again, the emphasis was on precision flying, including formation flying and blind flying practice in which one pilot was under the hood, concentrating on the flight instruments, and the other maintained a vigilant visual lookout. Mid-air collisions were infrequent, but potentially disastrous for the crews of both aircraft. The crew of one of our flying boats had a narrow escape when a Kingfisher scout plane ran its single float along the length of the main plane as it descended on an instrument letdown. The pilot of the scout plane landed upside down in the waters of the bay with his cockpit hatch jammed. The rescue boats that put off from shore were too late to free him.

We had three weeks of intensive practice in manoeuvering the P2Y-2 in the air and on the water. We found that although these big flying boats were easy to handle and graceful in the air, they took on a different characteristic when waterborne. They became like a powered sailboat, at the mercy of winds and tides, and required all the skills of seamanship that we could muster. For example, there were three ways of completing a flight: one could beach the aircraft on soft sand, or one could bring the aircraft to a landing ramp and be hauled ashore by a tractor, or, one could tie up to a mooring buoy and wait for a marine craft to ferry the crew ashore. The choice of method was dictated by many factors and required varying degrees of sailing and powerboat skills.

For instance, local geographical conditions could affect the size of the alighting and mooring areas. In the Pacific theatre of war, and in the Indian Ocean, many flying boat squadrons operated from coral atolls, with minimal docking or beaching facilities. In the absence of mooring buoys, the skipper of a flying boat would have to carry out anchoring procedures and maintain an anchor watch with half the crew aboard in case the wind changed in strength or direction. If the squadron was operating from the waters of a busy harbour, such as Gibraltar, or Plymouth, it might be impossible to beach or anchor, and crews and maintenance parties would have to be ferried by marine craft. Since a flying boat by definition is a craft that takes off from and lands on water, the pilot has to be experienced in determining how to resolve the particular problems presented by each individual alighting area.

In the sheltered waters and sunny skies of the Gulf Coast our instructors made sure that we were prepared for any given set of circumstances, and eventually we were ready for the final phase of our flying training at Pensacola, and were within sight of earning our wings.

Having mastered the basic elements of flying boat operations, we were now ready for the transition to an operational aircraft in current use by the Royal Air Force, the PBY-5, or the Consolidated Catalina as it was known in the RAF. The final weeks of our training consisted of navigation (both dead-reckoning and astral), gunnery, and bombing. Reality was added to our exercises by the knowledge that German U-boats were operating off the coast.

On operational flight exercises, we would take turns at manning different positions in the aircraft, carrying out various crew duties. Our typical training crew would consist of seven

TODAY MUST BE CHRISTMAS

men: staff pilot and aircraft captain, staff radio operator/ordnance man, and five cadets sharing the duties of copilot, navigator, front turret or bowman, waist gunner, and tunnel gunner.

On one such flight, I had been assigned to the tunnel position, which required that, once airborne, I open a floor hatch in the stern compartment, lock it open, and swing a .30 calibre Browning machine gun into position facing downwards and to the rear. We had been simulating a reconnaissance patrol, flying at 700 feet over the Gulf of Mexico, and the cadet navigator had just given the pilot a new course for the next leg of the patrol when John Bazalgette, a classmate in the front turret, called up on the intercom.

"Bowman to Captain," he drawled in his inimitable English Public School accent. "U-boat surfacing five degrees on the port bow, distance about three miles."

What happened next was unbelievable. Lieutenant Commander Hoyt threw the aircraft into a skidding turn and dived toward the submarine, yelling over the intercom: "There goes the goddamn son-of-a-bitch. Open fire!"

As we skidded over the U-boat's conning tower, the pilot released our two depth charges which fell wildly astern and to starboard of the periscope as the U-boat crashdived.

"Captain to Tunnel. Did we hit her? Can you see any wreckage?"

I clicked on my microphone. "Not a thing, sir. Only depth charge scum."

It was my first of the three encounters I had with U-boats during the next three years and I vowed to keep a cooler head than Commander Hoyt if ever I should be lucky enough to carry out an attack. John Bazalgette and I discussed the incident as we walked back from the hangar and he was inclined to be more charitable than I about the instructor's panic and loss of control.

"After all, old boy. Not many Yanks have seen much action

yet. It's only a few months since Pearl Harbor, and they're still getting over the shock."

I've thought about the incident many times over the years and I still think it was setting a poor example of operational efficiency to future aircraft captains. All that we had seen of the United States Navy to date had reinforced their deserved reputation for coolness under fire, and their emphasis on crew discipline. I was probably overly critical and saw the incident from the idealistic viewpoint of a young airmen barely nineteen years of age who had already seen more action than his American instructors.

The day I graduated from Squadron Four was a mixture of the ridiculous and the sublime. I took my completion certificate into the RAF Liaison Officer, a Flight Lieutenant, who looked up in boredom from his paper work. "I suppose you want your wings, do you? Get them sewn on right away and report to the Commandant's office at 09:00 hours tomorrow."

With that he opened his drawer and tossed over the coveted wings and a pair of sergeant's stripes. No congratulations. No fuss, no muss. I made allowances for the fact that he was a wingless wonder in the Administrative Branch, but couldn't help feeling a little put down. After all, I'd sweated through the past fifteen months to earn the damn things and it wouldn't have hurt to have made more of an occasion of this special rite of passage.

The next day's interview with the Commandant of the United States Naval Air Station, Pensacola, was completely different. Captain A.C. Reid was one of the earliest naval aviators and had commanded the first Atlantic crossing in an old NC-4 flying boat in 1919, four years before I was born. He was an imposing figure in his white dress uniform and personally congratulated the dozen or so American and British Flight Cadets gathered in his office, giving each one of us a firm handshake.

"Good luck, gentlemen. You're going to need it."

The date was May 14, 1942, and I was one month short of my nineteenth birthday. Recalling the emotions of the moment it seems that my overwhelming feeling was of preparedness to do the job, and an eagerness to be assigned to an operational squadron before the fighting was over. In my naivete I did not understand that there was yet more training ahead of me before I joined a Coastal Command squadron over six months later. Nor could I have known that the winter of 1942 would see the German U-boat fleet's sinking, of thousands of tons of Allied shipping and inflicting the most crippling losses that Britain was to suffer during the five years and nine months duration of the Battle of the Atlantic. There would be time enough for me to make my contribution.

Meantime I had a brief forty-eight hours to obtain all the necessary clearances which would release me from U.S.N.A.S. Pensacola, and to say farewell to the dear friends we had made in the city. There was a tearful farewell to Emma Glass and her family and friends. Promises to write were given and addresses exchanged. For all of us it was a wrench to say goodbye to those wonderful people whose homes we had shared and from whom we had enjoyed so much loving, caring, and unstinting hospitality.

As Farmer and I rolled northward in the train that was to take us back through Detroit to our next posting to RAF Ferry Command at Dorval, Montreal, we were absorbed in our own thoughts. My emotions were in turmoil. I wasn't sure if my feelings for Emma were deep enough to survive years of separation, or if her feelings for me were anything more than a romantic fantasy. I wondered if we could reconcile our different cultural backgrounds, and whether I would ever see Emma again. I knew Farmer was eager to get back to see his Margaret, the bride whom he had not seen for over a year. I was looking forward to seeing my family in London, but even more keen to get to Montreal, where, it was rumoured, we were to join ferry crews delivering one of the more than 900 Catalinas that would enable Coastal Command to increase its protection of Allied convoys and to hunt down German, Italian, and Japanese submarines all over the globe.

EIGHT

Ferry Command

Our RECEPTION AT RAF Ferry Command Headquarters at Dorval was rather an anticlimax. About twenty or so newly-graduated pilots were ushered into the office of Air Vice-Marshal Sir Frederick William Bowhill, Air Officer Commanding the newly-formed Ferry Command, who had just taken over from a civilian organisation known as ATFERO. Many of the experienced Canadian pilots were former airline captains or bush pilots who were qualified to fly several types of aircraft and who had had all weather experience over continental and transoceanic routes. Some of them were still civilians and we found it somewhat of an anomaly to be taking orders from them. AVM Bowhill had bushy eyebrows and seemed to have a cantankerous disposition to match.

"We don't have any accommodation for you here, so get yourselves digs in town. We'll give you a living-out allowance, but we don't want you hanging around here making a nuisance of yourselves. Come into the station every second Friday at 10:00 hours and pick up your pay. A shuttle bus will pick you up and drop you at Dominion Square. When you've found accommodation leave your address and phone number with the Orderly Room. And remember, don't call us, we'll call you."

Not exactly a delirious speech of welcome, but the sort of reception we were used to receiving in transit units. Farmer and I joined with another couple of our classmates, Phil and Brian, who had graduated with us, and we managed to find an inexpensive apartment on Côte-des-Neiges with a French Canadian lawyer and his family. The family occupied one half of a large four bedroom flat and they sublet to us two double rooms with a shared bathroom. The rent was ridiculously inexpensive, and even included a continental breakfast served in our rooms by the lawyer's attractive seventeen-year-old daughter, who flirted outrageously with all four of us. A few doors down the hill was a small Chinese laundry, and around the corner on St. Catherine Street we made friends with the owner of a Greek restaurant. A short distance up the hill on Sherbrooke Street, across from the Ritz Carlton Hotel, was a beautiful old home that had been converted into an air force club. Shortly after we arrived, we attended the formal opening and had the pleasure of meeting Air Marshal Billy Bishop, the famous Canadian air ace from the Great War, as well as Herbert Wilcox, the film director, and his beautiful wife, Anna Neagle, the popular English actress.

I recalled that as an eleven-year-old schoolboy collecting autographs, I had the nerve to ring the bell of her flat on Curzon Street and was tongue-tied when she opened the door. She had signed my autograph album, and was patient and kind then as she was now, although I was still too shy to remind her of our previous meeting.

The club was a haven for airmen away from their home countries and not only provided a comfortable place to while away the time between the occasional training flight, but also was a good place to meet people and to enjoy the hospitality of some of Montreal's leading families. The hostesses were all volunteers and brought together transient airmen and local families who wanted to invite guests to their dinner tables or to spend a weekend at a country cottage. In this way we came to learn something of old Montreal and the countryside around it. One of the hostesses was Betty Wilson, daughter of Doug Wilson, the former head of the Atlantic Ferry Organisation. She invited three of us to attend a gala evening at the Seagram family's elegant home and suggested I drive us all in the family car, a Packard Clipper. I had very little driving experience, having been taught to drive on my uncle's small Morris Eight, and having shared the ownership of a 1939 Ford sedan with Johnny and Farmer whilst we were at Pensacola.

Nothing daunted, however, I slid behind the wheel and steered the enormous boat-length automobile down Sherbrooke Street. Betty directed me and we had almost safely made it to the Seagram house when I clipped the curb with the rear wheel as I turned into the driveway. When we came out to drive home we found the rear tire was very flat, much to my embarrassment and my friends' amusement. The Wilson family was most generous and Betty's father merely remarked, "Of course, you chaps drive on the wrong side, don't you?"

At the party we met Chuck Adams, a civilian test pilot who had transferred from ATFERO to the Ferry Command Unit at Dorval. We told him of our interview with the Air Officer Commanding and he chuckled appreciatively.

"Don't listen to that stuffy old bastard. And don't let him keep you away from flying. Bring your helmet out to the airfield anytime and you can keep your hand in as co-pilot on test flights."

He was as good as his word and over the next couple of months we were able to fly with him as he carried out acceptance tests on aircraft as they were delivered from the United States. Not only did this experience prevent us from getting bored, but it also gave us useful practice on different types of aircraft. In this way I got to fly the Lockheed Hudson, which the RAF was using for coastal patrol duties, as well as the Consolidated Liberator, the B-24, which was later used to close the mid-Atlantic gap that hitherto had prevented land-based aircraft from giving trans-Atlantic convoys continuous air cover through their long and hazardous voyages.

Despite the pleasant diversions of Montreal, it was with great relief that I at last received the call to report to Ferry Command's base at Boucherville on the St. Lawrence River. I was to join a crew from 109 Squadron, RAF, that was being equipped with the Catalinas that were beginning to arrive in increasing numbers from the Consolidated plant in San Diego, via Elizabeth City, North Carolina. Our captain was a civilian pilot, who told us to address him as Mr. Williams, and made it clear to us that his priority was to get our Catalina across the Atlantic and into action as quickly as possible. He also made it clear to me that, as third pilot, my job was to stay out of his way and to make myself as useful as possible. Undeterred by his low expectations, I pitched in and made myself useful wherever I could—fending off the marine craft tender, assisting the rigger with mooring procedures, and deploying the drogues whenever the Captain called for them.

We were soon prepared for the short flight from Montreal to Gander Lake, Newfoundland, and took off on a clear sunny day in late August. Gander was a hive of activity in 1942 as the force of the American Lend-Lease plan began to gather momentum.

Weather held us fogbound for two nights and we took advantage of the lull by attending a Friday afternoon and evening party at the main base. The food was plentiful and I returned to our anchorage with a whole roast chicken, which I produced in the middle of our Atlantic crossing, causing our captain to revise his opinion of newly-graduated third pilots. Pilot Officer Wright, our Canadian radio officer, had also managed to bring a bowl of potato salad and some fresh pineapple, so it was something of an unusual feast that was being consumed in the cockpit as we cruised at 4,500 feet across mid-Atlantic in the small hours of the morning.

We made landfall at the Bloody Foreland and turned south along the west coast of Ireland until we reached the mouth of the Erne River where it flows into Donegal Bay. From there we turned east and flew over Innishmurray and into Lough Erne, where we landed after a flight of seventeen and three-quarter hours. A Walton dinghy came out to ferry us ashore and I joined the other NCOs in the crew for a hot meal in the Sergeant's Mess and a much needed sleep in one of the Nissen huts assigned to transient crews.

After a substantial breakfast of eggs, bacon, and fried potatoes, we took off again for Scotland, where we alighted on the River Clyde, and were given a warm welcome by Scotland's Customs Officers. When we arrived at the Customs Office to have our personal luggage examined, I was astonished to see tots of malt whisky lined up on the counter, one for each member of the crew. Mr. Williams picked up the first glass and addressed the Customs men.

"Here's tae us. Wha's like us. Damn few, and they're all daid." Then he turned to the rest of us and declared, "By the authority vested in me as a member of the Short Snorter's Club, I hereby appoint you all as Short Snorters. I want a dollar bill from each of you, which I will sign certifying you as members. Keep that bill with you at all times and if you hear someone claim that he has flown the Atlantic, challenge him to produce his membership card. If he can't, he buys drinks, but if he asks to see your bill and you haven't got it, you pay!"

So I was inducted into the prestigious Short Snorter's Club. Sad to say I have long since lost my dollar bill, but the likelihood that I shall be challenged by an old Short Snorter is dwindling with each year that passes. Of course, crossing the Atlantic by air is no longer the distinctive achievement it once was, as thousands of jet airliners criss-cross the Atlantic every year carrying passengers who think nothing more of the experience than of crossing the street.

NINE

Return of the Prodigal

I SAID FAREWELL TO THE BOYS of 109 Squadron, who were staying in Gourock for a few days while their Catalina was being equipped with new radar gear at Scottish Aviation, and to Mr. Williams, who was leaving the same day for Prestwick, where he would catch a westbound aircraft back to Canada. I was handed a travel warrant with orders to report to the Aircrew Reception Centre at Bournemouth, and caught the night train from Glasgow to Euston, with enough time for a quick stop at home on the way. The train was full of uniforms and, seats being at a premium, I settled for a corner of the corridor where I sat on my kit bag and dozed fitfully throughout the night.

As we pulled into London in the pale light of dawn, I was shocked at the condition of the city. Even making allowances for the fact that one gets the least attractive view of the backyards of row houses or the sterile aspects of council flats on the approaches to any of London's mainline stations, I was not prepared for the smoke, the bomb damage, and the desolation that had occurred in the fifteen months I had been away. Noel Coward composed the song "London Pride" in 1942, while sitting on a bench in one of London's railway stations after an air raid, as a tribute to the plucky Londoners who had adopted the motto "business as usual."

All I saw as I travelled to Victoria by the Tube was the pale faces of the families who had spent the whole night underground sheltering from the air raid, and the drooping shoulders of the weary civil defence wardens as they attempted to clear the platforms for the day's traffic. On the Southern Railway train from Victoria to Streatham I saw gaping holes in the tracks where tired road crews were hard at work attempting to restore normal service, and I noticed the number of what used to be neat semi-detached houses draped with tarpaulins and with windows covered with tarpaper. Some houses had disappeared altogether and others were mere heaps of rubble. As the train crossed the viaduct over Balham High Street I caught a glimpse of one of London's red double-decker buses almost swallowed in a bomb crater. I learned later that a bomb had penetrated the Tube the previous night and that eighty people had been killed.

I thought of the times I had intended to write home and hadn't. I thought also of the good life I had led in Canada and the United States, of the absence of food rationing, the cities brightly lit at night, and the abundance of luxury items like chocolates. It made me aware that war is harder in many respects for the civilian population than for the serving soldier, sailor or airman. At least we had regular rations, a roof over our heads, and sturdy clothing for our bodies. My sister, my mother, and my grandmother had to subsist on their combined meagre food rations, were never sure whether they would crawl out of the shelter one morning and find the house in ruins, and felt more than any of us the deprivation of clothes rationing. And we had the certain knowledge that we were able to be more than passive victims of the bombing and could do something active to bring the war to an end, though in the autumn of 1942 not one of us could guess when that might be.

I had about twelve hours before my train left for Bournemouth and, by good fortune, found Ruth, my sixteen-year-old sister, still at home having breakfast with my mother and grandmother. Dad was already at work driving one of London's trams, which amazingly still ran to schedule. Mother would be leaving shortly to work an eight-hour shift at a war factory that made emergency rubber dinghies for the RAF. Poor Gran was left at home all day by herself, nervously awaiting the next air raid warning.

My unexpected arrival seemed to throw everyone into confusion, and my mother's chief concern was that she did not have enough food in the house to offer me a meal. Although I was not entitled to draw a leave ration card, since I was technically in transit and not on official leave, I had packed in the top of my kit bag some luxuries I had had the foresight to buy before leaving Montreal: tins of corned beef, peaches, Canadian bacon, as well as several large bars of Toblerone Swiss Chocolate. In no time a fresh pot of tea was made, bacon was sizzling in the pan, and a couple of thick slices of fried bread were soaking up the hot bacon fat. During breakfast we tried to catch up with over a whole year of family history.

Auntie Lou had got married, had a baby, and had lost it in an air raid. Grandmother had been holding the baby in her arms when a bomb fell outside the shelter. Aunt Lou and Grandma were shaken but unhurt, but the baby had been killed by the blast. To add to Aunt Lou's grief, her husband had just arrived home from his unit on weekend leave and was opening the garden gate when the bomb exploded in the road behind him. His body was found in the branches of a tree in the garden of the house next door. I now understood the reason for Grandma's nervousness, my mother's edginess, and my sister's hyperactive forced cheerfulness, a condition that persisted long after the war's end and one that in later years was to be the cause of chronic digestive problems induced by the bombing.

My favourite uncle, Ernest, one of the first to be conscripted into the Royal Army Service Corps, had been recommended for a commision, and was at this very moment attending an Officer's Training Unit in Wiltshire. My best friend, Harry, with whom I had fantasized before the war about flying, he as an air-gunner and me as a pilot, had completed his gunnery training and had recently joined the crew of a Sunderland flying boat operating out of Pembroke Dock, in Wales.

I found it almost impossible to give them even a glimpse of my life in Canada and the United States, not because I couldn't articulate my impressions, but because their notions of North America were conditioned by the films showing in the local cinemas, mostly musicals with stars like Hope, Crosby, and Lamour, or the news reels by Pathe. Neither tended to portray the lives of everyday people like ourselves.

All too soon it was time for me to leave to catch my train, and our goodbyes were accompanied by hurried embraces and the promise of a longer period of disembarkation leave in the very near future.

On arrival at Bournemouth I reported to the Orderly Room Sergeant at the Reception Centre and found to my surprise that my name appeared on his posting list.

"You're in the wrong place, sir," he looked up from his clipboard. "You are to report to the Mess Secretary at the Officers' Mess, just down the road in the Highcliffe Hotel."

He handed me an envelope containing my commissioning documents and I walked out in somewhat of a daze. Apparently, a selection board that I had attended before leaving Pensacola had recommended me for a commission, but the British and U.S. Governments had agreed that all pilots were to graduate with the rank of sergeant, and that those recommended for commissions would not be promoted until they had returned to England.

The fact that my commission took effect from my graduation

date, 15 May, meant that I had accumulated four months of back pay, a healthy amount since my pay had now jumped to that of pilot officer. All that was necessary for me to access this treasure was my signature authorising the RAF to deposit 500 pounds to a bank account in my name in London.

This unexpected bounty, together with another 100 pounds uniform allowance, came as a pleasant surprise and resulted in a sudden change in my lifestyle. A representative of Austin Reed, the military tailors, was in attendance in the hotel's billiard room, and I was duly measured for a dress uniform in the RAF's blue barathea cloth, to be delivered within forty-eight hours. The tailor was also delighted to provide me with dress hat, shoes, socks, shirts, a cashmere sweater in air force blue, and a smart officer's raincoat. The accompanying entitlement of clothing coupons was more than enough to cover my modest needs. It mattered not that the total bill was almost twice the uniform allowance. An officer's credit was apparently guaranteed, and all that was required was a down payment, the balance to be paid monthly. I also discovered that there were stiff penalties if one did not honour one's financial commitments, and that tailor's bills, like mess bills, were expected to be paid by the tenth of each month.

The remainder of the week was spent under the gentle guidance of an elderly flight lieutenant, a veteran of the Great War, who tutored us in the gentle art of how to behave as officers and gentlemen. On Friday we paraded to learn that we had been granted a fortnight's leave, reminded how an officer was expected to behave in public, warned of the consequences of lapses of protocol and of the vigilance of the military police in London, and, finally, handed our leave and travel authorisation documents, and our precious ration cards for fourteen days, which, we discovered, were equivalent to a month's rations for civilians.

Less than a week after passing through London on my way

to Bournemouth I was sitting in a reserved seat and enjoying the luxury, comfort, yes, and the privilege, of travelling first-class as an officer in wartime England. I was still rather self-conscious of my new uniform with its brand new pilot's wings, the thin blue pilot officer's line on each sleeve, and the tiny gold VR at each lapel signifying that I was commissioned in the Volunteer Reserve. The only other occupant, a ruddy-faced, ro-tund and much be-ribboned army major in the opposite corner seat, leaned forward and smiled.

"Don't mind if I smoke, old boy?" He produced a large cher-rywood pipe, a flat tin of Erinmore flake tobacco, and a box of Swan Vestas matches.

"Not at all, sir," I replied, a little overawed that he should even ask.

"Off on a spot of well-earned leave, eh? You chaps certainly deserve it. Wouldn't have your job for all the tea in China. Lookin' forward to a bit of poodle-fakin' I suppose. Got a pop-sie in London, I'll bet."

I murmured that I was indeed visiting family and that I hoped to see a show or two. I wasn't sure just how much I ought to offer in the way of personal information, and was much relieved when he got his pipe going satisfactorily and opened the Daily Telegraph to the cryptic crossword page. I noticed with much admiration that he completed each clue in ink.

The train made good time and as we neared London I no-ticed that the barrage balloons were raised, a sure sign that a raid was in progress. As we rattled through the points at Clap-ham Junction a pair of Spitfires sped overhead, either in hot pursuit of a quarry or, more likely, going in to land at their base at Hornchurch.

I bade a deferential farewell to the major, picked up my leather holdall (another new acquisition from Austin Reed) and headed for the Underground station, and my connection to Victoria. As the train drew in to the platform at Streatham

South, the All Clear sounded and I stepped smartly down Streatham Vale towards our little semi-detached house on Hawkhurst Road.

To my delight I found my father at home, though looking more gaunt than I had remembered him, cheerful as ever and happy to see me again. Never a demonstrative man, he shook my hand warmly and was obviously proud when I took off my raincoat and displayed my new wings.

"Tell you what, son, let's go down to the Norbury Arms for a celebration. The women have gone to Croydon, and I don't have to go back to work today, because I worked the early shift. The pub doesn't close until two and we've got time for a game of darts. You don't need a raincoat."

I knew from the lift in his shoulders and the tone of his voice that the pub would be full on a Saturday afternoon and he wanted to show me off to the locals. For my part I was glad to fall in with his suggestion. We'd seen little enough of each other since the outbreak of war and I knew how much he enjoyed his pint of bitter and his game of darts. He was not a heavy drinker and often made a pint last all evening, but he was a wickedly accurate dart player. I knew that we would be able to beat all comers and as soon as he'd bought our drinks he chalked his initials on the scoreboard and we became the challengers of the winners of the game in progress.

When our turn came up he took the first throw and with his first dart found the 'double top,' the outer ring of the twenty. His next two darts fell cleanly into the triple twenty ring and we were off to an impressive start, 160 scored. At our local darts club custom dictated that the winners win the best of three games of 301 points, starting and finishing on a double. We had a remainder of 141 points to get. Their first man missed the double top by a hairsbreadth, his dart pitched a fraction too high, but his next dart found the double nineteen, his third the triple seventeen. Eighty-nine scored, 212 left. I took my stance on the mark, took a deep breath and exhaled slowly. My first dart fell in the centre of the twenty, the second found the triple nineteen and the third landed with a satisfying thunk in the triple eight. 101 scored, double top left for Dad. Our other opponent was a dark horse. All his three darts found the triple twenty. They needed a double sixteen. Dad raised his first dart and with a quick flick of his wrist he found double top. First game to us.

The second game went to our opponents when I missed an easy shot at the double sixteen, but we finished our third game in grand style when Dad opened with a bull centre and then dropped two darts into the triple twenty, leaving me to find 131. I could feel Dad watching me, but I dared not look at him, instead concentrating all my attention on the board. I aimed for the triple seventeen and held my breath until the dart found its mark, then exhaled slowly and took aim again. Eighty left, how best to go? Stay with the twenties and keep it even, but be sure to leave Dad with a double. My second dart fell easily in the centre of the triple twenty, and without hesitating I went straight for the double ten. Game over in six darts!

I looked across to Dad and he smiled quietly and raised his empty glass. He didn't say a word, but I knew by the relaxed set of his shoulders how proud he was of me. I drained my glass and raised my empty glass in salute. We were closer then than we had ever been before and I wanted to tell him how much I loved him, but I didn't know how, so we stood there smiling at each other until our opponents broke the intimate moment with "Same again?" We both nodded and prepared to face the next pair of challengers. As their first man took the mark, Dad came over and said, "We've got time for one more game before closing time. You all right?"

"Fine," I said. I wanted to hug him but the moment had passed.

When we got home, my mother and sister were in the

kitchen putting the groceries away, while Gran had settled down for an afternoon nap. When I stood in the doorway Mum looked at my new uniform and caught me by surprise with her question.

"What are you wearing that for?"

"It's my uniform."

"It's not the one you wore last week."

"No, I've been commissioned."

"What did you want to do that for?"

I was stunned. I knew that my mother had not wanted me to go to grammar school, and had argued that we couldn't afford to accept the London County Council Scholarship. I had heard her quarelling with my father on that occasion that going to a posh school was putting on airs and why wasn't the ordinary school good enough for their kids? I couldn't understand her attitude. Both my Dad and my sister were so obviously proud of my achievements and my mother's remarks wounded my feelings. Strange how little incidents like this can cause irreparable damage to family relationships, how mere words can sever the most intimate connections and leave gaps that can never be bridged. Sadly, this rift between us remained until the day of her death. Would that we could take back words that wound, or better yet leave them unspoken.

The war that we had been told would be over by Christmas 1939 had now lasted three years and its effects were showing on the civilian population, especially in the larger cities where air raids were almost a nightly occurrence. In September of 1942 there was not much to be cheerful about either at home or abroad. The Nazi flag flew over most of Europe, the Allies had suffered great losses in the Battle of the Atlantic, in the Middle East, and on the Russian Front. In the Far East, Hong Kong and Singapore had fallen and the United States was still reeling from the aftermath of Pearl Harbor.

In London a great effort was being made to carry on as usual,

but everyone was weary of the war, of the deprivation, of all the inconveniences, the rationing and the incessant air raids. I hadn't realised just how much it affected the ordinary family until I spent those two weeks on leave in 1942.

Routinely, supper would be a rushed affair with everyone listening for the distant sounds of sirens. My sister, Ruth, was generally the first to detect that far-off wavering note, and immediately started to organise Grandma for her nightly trip down the garden path to the Anderson shelter that had been sunk in what used to be our lawn.

Fortunately, my father and I had been at home to dig the hole and to assemble the corrugated iron sections so that the local council could pour a concrete floor and Dad and I could then cover the shelter with two feet of packed earth. I think we all knew that it would provide no protection against a direct hit, but it was certainly better than having the house collapse on you. At first, poor old Gran used to protest vociferously at the mere idea of spending the night in a gloomy underground cave, but after Dad and I gave the interior a coat of white enamel paint, built in some narrow bunk beds, and installed an electric light and a small Valor stove, she was persuaded, with not a little grumbling, to take her appointed place each night. But she insisted that her prize possession, an old brown betty teapot, should always accompany her. I found the nights in the shelter claustrophobic and felt responsible for the safety of the family, my father generally being away driving his tram through the air raids, or walking home from the other side of the river when his shift was over.

TEN

Operational Training

I WASN'T SORRY WHEN MY LEAVE came to an end and I reported to my new unit in the little market town of Harrogate, Yorkshire, where I would be taking a general reconnaisance course, preparatory to joining a flying boat squadron in Coastal Command. Most of our classes took place at the old Empire Hotel, at the foot of the town, near the Royal Spa.

Harrogate is a pretty town with well-kept municipal parks and gardens, and gently winding streets with many tea shops and cafes. This part of Yorkshire was largely agrarian and, lacking any sizeable industrial plants, was little troubled by air raids. Because of its location in rich farmlands there were other not-so-obvious but neverthless tangible advantages. Rationing was the same for everyone, town or country, but there were always little extras to be had in rural England, like the occasional rabbit or a thick slice of pork pie with your pint of ale in the local pub. Beer was plentiful, although short drinks were quickly exhausted and Scotch whisky was at a premium. Most landlords would keep their Scotch for the men in uniform, but as time went by there was less and less of the golden liquid to be had unless you were a regular customer or a good friend of the innkeeper.

Most of our days were spent in the classroom down in the Empire Hotel and our evenings were spent at the other end of town in our rooms at the Queen's Hotel, resolving complex navigational problems that required the dead-reckoning calculation of the maximum time that could be spent escorting a convoy, given a certain maximum all up weight of fuel and armament, extreme marginal weather conditions at the take-off point, as well as the distinct possibility of being diverted to land hundreds of miles from base at the end of a long patrol. Much as we tried to rationalise that nothing quite so dire could happen to us, I think we all knew that it was better to be prepared for the worst. Just as well, for the worst was yet to come and we were soon to come face to face with reality in the Battle of the Atlantic.

At the end of our course a dance was held in the Officers' Mess to celebrate the completion of one course and the arrival of the next batch. Those of us who had been in residence for six weeks had the advantage over the newcomers when it came to finding dance partners, and I took the opportunity to ask a tall, blonde WAAF officer if she would accompany me. Cynthia was in charge of the small WAAF contingent that provided support to the school. Most of the girls in blue worked in the transport pool, in the Orderly Room, or in the Mess as waiters, cooks, or batwomen. She was referred to as the Queen Bee, and although she came into our mess for her lunch and dinner she was allowed to live at home with her father, a country doctor, who had a rambling old house out on the Otley road.

I wasn't much of a dancer but the evening went moderately well and around midnight she asked me to walk home with her. As we passed through the hotel's revolving door, she hesitated, bent down to pick up something, handed me a warm and silky bundle, and said with a perfectly straight face, "Put those in your pocket for me." I had no idea what had happened but, since I was already carrying her evening purse, I slipped the garment in my greatcoat pocket. "Damned wartime cami-

knickers, no elastic, only one button. One yank and they're off."
I blushed as I realised what I was carrying in my pocket, but she
was quite at ease during the long walk home. When we reached
her garden gate she kissed me chastely on the cheek and retrieved her possessions from my pocket. "Thanks for a lovely
evening," she said, and was gone. As I walked back along the
country road I was in a state of wonderment. Wondering if it
had really happened, and if there was something else expected
of me. I was still wondering when I fell asleep. The next morning I was wakened by a batwoman bringing me my morning
tea.

"Did you have a nice time at the dance, sir? Saw you dancing
with our officer, Miss Cynthia. She isn't half pretty, isn't she?
And so much fun, too."

I mumbled something about enjoying myself and, yes, it had
been fun, then busied myself with finishing my packing. Later
that day, as I sat in the train rolling south to Gloucestershire, I
wondered whether my encounter with Miss Cynthia had been
some kind of test of chivalry.

I arrived at Number 3 (Pilots) Advanced Flying Unit which
was located on a field at Long Newnton, a satellite of the main
base at South Cerney. It was the beginning of November and
the weather had begun to deteriorate, or rather, winter weather
in Southern England was making every flight a challenge. We
were introduced to our aircraft, the Airspeed Oxford, a twin-
engined monoplane which had been built by a company
owned by the author Neville Shute. It was not particularly difficult to fly, but was a bit skittish if you came in for a landing
with more than the recommended airspeed. To make matters
more interesting there were no runways, just a circle of grass.

The main purpose of the course was to provide graduates of
the Empire Training Programme with experience of flying in
marginal weather conditions, and in particular in finding our
way around the British Isles with relatively few navigational

aids. My first reminder of the joys of flying in winter came when we had suffered almost a week of endless rain, which turned the airfield into a morass, followed by a sharp cold snap when the mud turned solid, leaving the surface of the field like a skating rink. After a brief familiarisation flight, and a check flight with the chief flying instructor, I was authorised to carry out circuits and landings for an hour and a half. According to the weather forecaster, the cloud base was at a 1,000 feet, and visibility was three miles, with only a slight chance of intermittent rain or snow. In fact, I found myself flying the circuit at 700 feet through heavy snow showers, with the visibility never better than half a mile. The result was that I was forced to carry out a 'bad weather circuit,' flying out of sight of the runway mainly on the gyro compass, and relying on accurate rate turns to bring me in on a path that was lined up with the wind direction. There were no airfield lights and the only feature that distinguished the airfield from any other piece of pasture land was the circular perimeter track that encompassed the landing area.

I had barely time to complete the pre-landing check and straighten out from the final turn when I saw the boundary of the field racing towards me. I had flaps and wheels down but my speed was too high for the frozen surface.

Ignoring the maxim 'when in doubt, go round again,' I cut the throttles and went sailing over the frozen grass and made a respectable 'wheeler,' touching down smoothly on the main

wheels. However, I still had plenty of speed and found that my efforts to brake had little effect. Disc brakes had not been introduced at this time and the old type of drum brake was not very effective, particularly when the wheels were splashing in and out of freezing mud. Realising that I was rapidly running out of grass, and the perimeter track was looming up fast, I applied maximum brake and prayed that something would stop me from barreling through the hedge and through the ditch at the far end of the field. Miraculously, the starboard wheel locked and caught on the perimeter track, and the plane spun neatly through ninety degrees. I released the brake a fraction and continued at a fast taxi speed through the dispersal area and back to the take-off point. I couldn't know that the chief flying instructor was watching from the window of the flight office, but when I returned to the hangar after completing several rather more sedate landings he was waiting for me. I had just completed the Form 700, the aircraft maintenance record, when Squadron Leader Brown spoke over my shoulder.

"Where did you learn to fly like that? We don't need hotshot pilots, we want airframe drivers who respect their aircraft and bring them back in one piece."

I was about to point out that I had indeed brought the aircraft back in one piece, but decided that discretion was the better part of valour.

"Sorry, sir. Came in too fast on the first landing and should have gone 'round again. It won't happen again."

"Never mind, as long as you learn from your mistakes. Otherwise is the aircraft serviceable?"

"Yes, sir. They're just filling the tanks."

"Good. Don't bother to change. I want you to come with me over to South Cerney. We'll be back in time for dinner."

I speculated as to the nature of our flight. Was it an additional check flight to reassure him that I was safe to fly solo in the Oxford? Or was he about to recommend my suspension from flying training? When he motioned me to sit in the right hand seat I was even more mystified. He didn't need a co-pilot for the twenty minute flight to South Cerney. What, then?

"Don't get much opportunity for flying for sheer pleasure. Circuits and landings get a bit boring after a while. Thought you might like to have a look at the German Flying Circus that's visiting Cerney."

Even more mysterious. What flying circus? Did he say German?

We flew over the old Roman villa at Chedworth and as I looked down onto the ruins it seemed hard to believe that a foreign military presence had occupied English soil nearly 2,000 years ago. When we joined the circuit at South Cerney there seemed to be an unusual amount of ground activity near the control tower. As we taxied past the tower towards the visitors' parking area I saw that there were indeed three aircraft with distinctive German markings parked close together: a Junker's 88, a Focke Wolfe 190, and a Heinkel 111, like the one that had carried out a low-level attack on Cranwell when I was there over a year ago. But what were they doing here? As though he could read my mind the squadron leader turned in his seat and grinned at me.

"Let's go have a look-see. Apparently these aircraft were all captured in perfect flying condition and have been sent to Central Flying School for testing and evaluation. Trouble is, they have to

go everywhere with a Spitfire escort so that trigger happy airfield defence gunners don't shoot them down. Let's see if we can have a dekko inside one of them."

We strolled over to the Heinkel and Squadron

Leader Brown greeted a wing commander in battle dress, carrying both the Distinguished Flying Cross and the Air Force Cross below his wings.

"What brings you to Gloucestershire, John? Decided to move over to the opposition?"

The wing commander smiled. "No, Larry. The Air Ministry thought it might be a good idea if some of our pilots could get a closer look at what we're up against. Want to come up and see how she handles? We can't leave the circuit without our escort, but you can try a couple of touch-and-go landings. Bring your friend here."

When I realised that he meant me I needed no persuading to follow them into the Heinkel. As I stood behind the two pilots and looked at the strange instrument panel I realised that, apart from the fact that all readings were in German, the flying instruments were familiar and the layout of the controls was similar to that of the Oxford. The one thing that was distinctly different was the rumble of the two Junker's Jumo motors as we taxied out to the take-off point. South Cerney boasted new concrete runways and we paused before moving onto the threshold of the active runway until we had received a green light from the tower. Radio traffic was kept to a minimum and restricted to messages of a strictly operational nature. When we received visual permission to take off, the Wing Commander let the Heinkel roll forward, locked the tail wheel, and opened up the throttles to take-off power. I had a great view as we sped down the runway and after a short run we were airborne and climbing steadily to circuit height. The heavy aircraft seemed to have plenty of power and responded readily to the controls. After one circuit and a touch-and-go landing the wing commander handed over control to Brown who made three very smooth landings. Then Brown turned to me and made a gesture for me to take his place.

"Sorry I can't let you land the thing, but try a quick circuit and approach and I'll take over for the touchdown. Not that

you can't manage it, but I can't risk bending this one. It's the only airworthy one we've got."

I was eager to fulfil his confidence in my flying and concentrated on maintaining accurate height and heading. He carried out the pre-landing check and I made the turn on to the final approach and saw the green Very light come sailing up towards us from the control tower. As I brought the Heinkel in over the boundary the wing commander placed his hands gently on the controls and nodded to me.

"I have control," he said.

"You have control, sir," I answered, and relaxed in my seat as we rounded out for the touchdown. As we taxied back to the hangar I reflected that there weren't many pilots who had flown a German bomber before flying on operations against the enemy.

Thankfully, the weather improved enough to enable our course to finish just before Christmas. A notice went up on the Orderly Room bulletin board showing our postings to operational squadrons. I was the only one listed to travel overseas, to Number 202 (Coastal) Squadron based at Gibraltar.

ELEVEN

Battle of the Atlantic
(Part 1)

MY TRAVEL WARRANT TOOK me to the embarkation point, West Kirby, just outside Liverpool, and within forty-eight hours I was travelling south on board a troopship bound for North Africa. The Monarch of Bermuda carried mainly American troops to reinforce the Tunisian campaign, but also carried a small party of RAF personnel that were to join the Gibraltar garrison.

There were about eighty ships in the convoy and we followed the ten degree West line of longitude in order to keep out of range of the Junker's 88s based at Brest. Unfortunately, we were still within range of the Focke Wolfe 200 long-range shipping raiders that ranged almost to mid-Atlantic and radioed information concerning Allied convoys to the U-boat wolf packs on station just off the Bay of Biscay. The British Officer Commanding Troops asked for volunteers to man the oerlikon cannon turrets so that the ship's gunnery crews could be augmented with those of us who were trained in the recognition of enemy aircraft. It was certainly better than trying to find a place to sit below decks, where every space seemed to be taken up with American infantrymen and their officers engrossed in seemingly endless games of poker in which huge fortunes were being made and lost.

It was with some irony that my watch reported the presence of two aircraft shadowing the convoy on opposite sides, one of them a FW 200, the other an RAF Catalina from my new squadron. The Catalina was much slower than the Focke Wolfe and it was frustrating to see the two aircraft keeping station on either side of the convoy. Of course, the pilot of the Catalina could not hope to take on the four-engined Focke Wolfe, being not only out-performed in speed but also being faced with a much heavier armed aircraft equipped with 20 mm cannon in power-operated turrets. Still, it was irksome to see the German raider reverse course and circle away from the Coastal Command escort aircraft whenever the Catalina attempted to close the gap. Of course, neither aircraft would dare to cut across the convoy, both having a profound respect for the accuracy of the Royal Navy gunners on the surface escorts.

The convoy was fortunate in not losing any of its number and it was with some relief that we rounded Cape St. Vincent at dawn of the fourth day and discovered we had lost our German shadow. We steamed through the Straits of Gibraltar where the convoy dispersed and the Monarch of Bermuda picked up new escort ships to see us safely into harbour at Oran where the American troops were disembarked.

The OC Troops detailed me to be in charge of a party of other ranks who were granted six hours shore leave. Three sergeants belonging to the Black Watch were rejoining their regiment on Gibraltar and were assigned to assist me to keep tabs on this mixed bag of some forty-five soldiers, sailors and airmen who were all bound for the Rock. The NCOs carried Sten guns and for the first time I wore my side arm, a long-barreled .38 Smith and Wesson service revolver. By the time I came down the gang plank the senior NCO, an RAF flight sergeant, had formed the motley crew into three columns with the Senior Service on the right, the Army in the centre, and the RAF bringing up the rear. I brought the parade to attention, gave the command to right turn and took my position at the head of the column, followed by the flight sergeant. The three Black Watch sergeants took their place at the rear of the column, slinging their Sten guns over their shoulders.

I was feeling the weight of my responsibility for these fifty men, and was conscious of all eyes upon us as we marched through the dockyard gates, but I kept my eyes to the front and listened to the satisfying crunch of fifty pairs of army boots as we marched into town. We came to the main street that ran through town and I noticed that the men were marching with a lighter step. It was not until I looked back that I realised that half of our column was missing, and I was just in time to catch sight of three of the sailors disappearing into a bar. Still keeping step, I turned to the flight sergeant and was about to say something when he forestalled my question.

"Don't worry, sir. We'll pick them all up on the way back. When there's no one left but you and me and the Jocks, we'll stop for a beer ourselves."

It was then that I learned that field training of inexperienced young officers like myself was by tradition in the hands of senior NCOs in the Army and the Royal Air Force, and the Chief Petty Officers in the Royal Navy. As soon as the four sergeants and myself were the only ones left they steered me into a little French bistro and ordered bottles of beer for us all. The next couple of hours passed pleasantly enough, but when we stepped outside into the bright sunshine and started back to the dockyard the beer began to take effect on me.

I cannot recall too much of the march back to the ship, save that I do remember the flight sergeant whispered in my ear as we arrived at our berth.

"You give the command 'Leave Party, Halt,' on the right foot, sir. Then 'Into Line, Left Turn,' and hand them over to me. I'll do the rest, sir."

I managed to get the two commands in the right order and called the flight sergeant to dismiss the troops. He saluted me, winked his eye, then turned about to face the parade.

"Officer on parade. Leave party. Diiiiismiss!"

The parade turned smartly to the right, saluted, and broke ranks. The OC Troops was waiting at the top of the gang plank and returned my salute.

"Well done, Robertson. Never thought you'd bring them all back alive!"

Thankfully, I managed to find my way to my cabin and collapsed on my bunk. When I awoke at midnight I could hear the throb of the ship's screws as we steamed our way back to Gibraltar. Dawn found us at anchor in Algeciras Bay where a ship's tender took us and our baggage into the harbour. By this time my head had cleared and I was thrilled at the sight of the east face of the Rock of Gibraltar that housed a garrison of some 17,000 troops.

I reported to Wing Commander "Uncle" Case, Commanding Officer of 202 Squadron and he put me at ease by his evident pleasure at getting a replacement pilot.

"You'll be flying with Harry Sheardown. His second dickey is going back to Northern Ireland to take a Captain's Course at Killadeas next week, so you'd better learn all you can from him. I'll get the Adjutant to put you in his room so that they can give you your early calls together. Get your things stowed away and I'll meet you in the Mess for lunch and introduce you to them. They got back from a trip late last night so they're on standdown today. They'll probably want to take you in to town to show you around and introduce you to some of the local dens of iniquity."

At lunch I met some of the other squadron members, including

Dennis Briggs who had just received the DFC. His aircraft had located the German battleship Bismarck after it had sunk the battleship Hood and eluded the Royal Navy and Royal Air Force units that had been searching for it.

Operational flying as a Coastal Command second pilot in the next six months was to add to the experience I had accumulated at Pensacola, with Ferry Command, on the General Reconnaissance Course, and on the Advanced Flying School, and was to prepare me for the time when I, too, would be sent to complete my training as a flying boat captain.

202 Squadron was equipped with PBY Catalinas very similar to the aircraft I had learned to fly at Pensacola, with a few minor modifications. The upper part of the hull and the main planes were painted the colour of the waters over the North Atlantic and a modified form of the RAF roundel, consisting of two rings, red and blue, appeared on the wings and fuselage. The squadron had just been supplied with the new Mark VIII radar installation, but the basic configuration remained the same. The power plants were the old reliable Pratt & Whitney Twin Wasps and maximum speed (in a steep dive) was 212 knots. Take-off speed was sixty to sixty-five knots, depending on the surface conditions, climbing speed was eighty knots, and cruising speed was eighty-five to ninety knots. The cruising settings depended on the desired fuel consumption and whether the aircraft was being flown for maximum range (distance) or maximum endurance (longest time in the air). A good flight engineer and an experienced pilot could obtain maximum endurance with the pitch controls set to a shade under 1700 RPM and a throttle setting to maintain eighty knots airspeed. With a fuel capacity of 1,670 Imperial gallons and a consumption of sixty GPH it was possible to remain aloft for more than twenty-seven hours.

During the first three months with Harry Sheardown and his crew I learned that Coastal Command's biggest enemy was not the German U-boats but the winter weather. Most of our patrols reached far out into the Atlantic and demanded accurate flying and good navigation.

Moose, our Canadian navigator, was more than up to the challenge. Even in the foulest weather, with the aircraft wallowing around a convoy at eighty-three knots, our maximum endurance speed, he was tireless. Like the Captain, he was unable to take a break, but was continually at work, plotting our course, keeping his dead-reckoning log up to date, and advising the skipper of our position. When we were on station with a convoy his work never stopped, and on those rare occasions when we made contact with a U-boat he was responsible for drafting the sighting report which was radioed back to Coastal Command Headquarters. Harry Sheardown obviously trusted Moose's long experience which had earned him the deserved position of Squadron Navigation Leader. I only hoped that I would be fortunate to find such an outstanding navigator for my own crew. I learned from Moose's example the importance of keeping accurate charts and of maintaining a neat log.

I learned also that neatness and tidiness was every crew member's responsibility. Even though the interior cabins of the Catalina were spacious enough under normal conditions, by the time nine or ten crew members were aboard, together with the necessary gear and supplies, every little bit of storage space became a precious commodity. Accordingly, each individual had his own personal habit for stowing the materials he needed at hand. The navigator carried a bag crammed with instruments and his log sheets, together with his bubble sextant for taking sun or star sights.

Moose's navigation table was sacrosanct, and we all knew better than to rest anything on its orderly surface, even for a second. Our rigger had learned early not to place a mug of soup or coffee anywhere near Moose's precious charts or his navigation log. Each section of the hull was separated by water-tight bulkheads, but it was hard to keep the elements from pervading our living quarters. Even the most diligent of crews was hard pressed to keep water from accumulating in the bilges.

Frequently, when we were forced to taxi our flying boat from our moorings out through the anchored merchant shipping, it was almost impossible for the skipper to avoid taking water over the bows where it was caught in the swirl of the propellers and flung into every crack and crevice of the hull. Worse, when the skipper was trying to navigate between anchored shipping at night, the second pilot had to stand with his head through the roof hatch, aiming the steady beam of the Aldis lamp to guide him clear of anchor cables and large mooring buoys. Then, the water cascaded into the cockpit and drenched both pilots with cold sea water. It was no fun for the unfortunate second pilot, who bore the brunt of the drenching and who had no alternative but to sit in his wet flying gear until it dried on him.

Once the take-off point was reached and all hatches were closed, the pilots could concentrate on the take-off run itself. Algeciras Bay is only partly sheltered and is large enough to experience a range of surface conditions, from a light chop with light winds and clear visibility to a heavy swell with strong cross winds and driving rain. Often the worst conditions prevailed when we had to make a night take-off with a maximum fuel load and three depth charges under each wing. The strength of both pilots was sometimes needed to keep the heavy yoke pulled into their chests so that the aircraft would ride up on its stepped hull in order to reduce the flying spray.

On these occasions it was with great relief that we felt the rattle of the waves on the hull cease and we knew our thirty ton craft had become airborne. The tension began to lessen as the crew retrieved scattered equipment and went about their normal routine. The skipper levelled off the aircraft just below the cloud base and reduced the throttle settings and propeller pitch to obtain best cruising power. The flight engineer adjusted the mixture controls to give maximum range and started keeping a log of petrol and oil consumption.

As our heavily laden aircraft wallowed along at a sedate ninety knots, the gunners moved to their stations and began a visual lookout that would be maintained throughout the remainder of the patrol. My job as second pilot was to mapread our path along the Spanish coast by whatever means was available in the prevailing weather. Sometimes we had barely rounded the headland that marked the northern shoreline of the Straits of Gibraltar and identified the flashing light of Ceuta when the visibility closed right down and we were flying blind over the Atlantic on a course for Cape St. Vincent. At such times it was with some irony that we would recall the meteorological briefing that we had listened to only a scant hour before.

"The forecast for transit to the patrol area is for scattered low cloud, clearing occasionally to five-eighths cover, and with westerly winds moderate to strong, gusting to gale force as you approach the convoy's position. Conditions at base are fair for take-off, but deteriorating during the day, with the probability of heavy swell setting in from the southwest, giving marginal conditions for landing."

The met man's opening remarks would be met with derisive chuckles from the skippers and navigators. "Have you looked out of the window lately?"

Invariably, the response was the same: "Pull the blinds down! Take off, I say. I'll take the risk."

It was not until we made our first U-boat sighting that I really appreciated the value of a good navigator. We were escorting a convoy about 300 miles west of Lisbon when we were signalled by lamp from the Senior Naval Officer of the Convoy reporting an under-water contact from a destroyer ten miles ahead of the convoy and asking us to investigate. Moose immediately passed a new course to steer to the cockpit, and I set the course on the P.4 compass. We were flying in and out of cloud at 900 feet and Harry reduced power, descended to 700 feet and turned on to the new heading. Just then the front gunner reported a U-boat on the surface dead ahead and the skipper sounded the klaxon horn to alert the crew. By the time we had turned on to the U-boat's track, Moose had poked his head into the cockpit to confirm that a sighting report was on its way.

At about the same time the U-boat started to crash dive and, as we made our attack from the stern, the conning tower was almost submerged. Harry made a steady approach at the recommended speed of 120 knots and a height of 200 feet and pressed the button to release the six 250 lb. depth charges we carried under our wing racks. At this stage of the war there was no low-level bomb sight in service in Coastal Command flying boats and all U-boat attacks were made visually with the pilot estimating the point of release. I glanced out of the hatch on my side at the wing racks and was horrified to see the depth charges still in place. As often happened, the electrical release mechanism had failed us.

"Blast! Pilot to Navigator. I'm going to climb up and fly into the sun on this heading for thirty minutes. Drop a marine marker and give me a time to turn and a course to intercept the U-boat on its last known track."

"Roger, skipper. Marker and smoke flares dropped. Time to turn 1805Z. I'll have your new heading in a moment."

Harry was using his head and guessed that the U-boat would surface again to attack the convoy once its commander was assured the coast was clear, particularly since he had not heard any depth charge explosions. Harry's bet was that we would be less likely to be spotted if we approached from the west with the sunset behind us, and he was right. Twenty minutes after our turn on to a reciprocal course the U-boat surfaced on our starboard beam.

Once more we went in to attack and this time I operated the

bomb distributor switch manually when Harry gave the nod. To our relief the depth charges fell along the U-boat's track with the third and the fourth straddling the conning tower. Harry swung the aircraft around in a steep bank, the port blister gunner began firing with his machine gun, the exploding depth charges sent plumes of water high in the air, and the nose gunner opened up with his twin Brownings. Meantime Moose had been busy taking photographs with our hand-held F.24 camera and had already given the radio operator an attack report to send. It was my first lesson in the crew discipline needed to press home a successful U-boat attack.

The last light had almost faded in the western sky as we made contact with the SNCO and I flashed a signal with our Aldis lamp, notifying him of the U-boat's last known position and of our successful attack.

Immediately the acknowledgement was flashed: CONGRATS. YOU BOYS HAVE ALL THE FUN. WILL SEARCH FOR INCRIMINATING EVIDENCE.

I flew the aircraft while Harry signalled that we were at the end of our fuel endurance and that we were returning to base. He ended his message with a quotation: AND FLIGHTS OF ANGELS SEE THEE TO THY REST.

They replied: YOU TOO. HAVE ONE FOR US WHEN YOU GO ASHORE.

I learned later that the Royal Navy required convincing evidence before it would confirm a claim that a U-boat had been sunk. Patches of oil and debris were not enough, since submariners on both sides would try to fool their pursuers by discharging waste from their torpedo tubes. When I asked what the Navy considered to be 'convincing,' I was told that the best evidence was usually in the form of human lungs that were retrieved from the wreck location. With no such tangible evidence, the result of our attack was assessed as only 'a probable damage,' but at least we had the satisfaction of giving one

U-boat crew a scare that had in all likelihood prevented an attack on the convoy. This may seem small reward for the long hours spent on patrol, when hour after hour passed without our sighting anything but the endless ocean. As someone succinctly described our war, it consisted of long periods of boredom punctuated by brief moments of fearful excitement.

The chances of sighting a U-boat travelling at periscope level were slight, the spume of spray that was sent up by the thin mast being practically indistinguishable from a breaking wave, and the North Atlantic was full of those. It was for that very reason that our lives were geared to routine. Each crew member had an allotted primary task, that of maintaining a keen visual watch from his position in the aircraft: the front gunner searched ahead and a sector forty-five degrees on either side of the fore and aft line; the two pilots concentrated on the sector from ahead to the port or starboard beam; the flight engineer, perched in his little seat in the tower that supported the mainplane, covered either beam; the waist gunners had the best view, since their canopies projected from the hull, and covered the two stern sectors, port and starboard; and, in the extreme tail position, the tunnel gunner could cover directly below and astern.

In addition to these seven visual observers, the radar operator had the ability to scan ahead and on either beam, according to which antennas were selected. But the early radar equipment was not always reliable and even if a contact appeared on the screen it was more often than not obscured in the 'mush' or ground return from the sea's surface. The ninth member of the crew, the radio operator, would be maintaining a listening watch on the Coastal Command frequency. In practice, there were three wireless operator/air gunners to share the visual watch—two gunners who were also flight engineers, and a solitary gunner who was an airframe fitter by trade. He dealt with such important functions as mooring or anchoring, as well as maintaining the rigging and controls. These nine, sometimes ten, specialist crew members were also capable of carrying out other duties if necessary. For example, the navigator acted as the bomb aimer and was also trained on the Browning machine guns; both pilots were qualified navigators, frequently took star sights for the navigator, could operate the radar, and in an emergency could man the guns. This overlap of duties produced a well-knit crew.

In this way, too, each crew developed its own way of dealing with standard operating procedures and routine drills, and after a time it was possible to see an aircraft touch down and as it approached the mooring area to identify the captain and his crew by the way they tied up at the buoy. Some skippers preferred their rigger to stay inside the front turret until the last moment, others would have him stand on the small coaming, or step, and hook his safety harness to a ring bolt. Other captains invariably had the waist gunners standing by with drogues, to slow the flying boat's forward progress. One of our captains insisted that his co-pilot monitor the mooring by standing on his seat with the upper half of his body through the top hatch, exposed to the weather, a particularly uncomfortable position since the two propellers were whirling around just behind the luckless co-pilot's head. A lot depended on the aircraft captains' disposition. Some were considerate of their crews and some were not.

Some thought it was part of a co-pilot's preparation for command to be subjected to the same discomforts as the crew. Whatever the personality of the captain or the composition of the crew, the common aim was to achieve as high a level of vigilance as possible over the long hours of an extended patrol. It was fitting, therefore, that No. 202 Squadron's crest bore a mallard drake and the legend 'Semper Vigilate.'

A typical patrol would begin with a crew call, say at 02:45 hours. An operational breakfast was served in the messes half an hour later and consisted of Gibraltar's 'dos huevos,' bacon, baked beans, toast, and coffee. The captain, navigator, and wireless operator would meet in the briefing room at 03:45 hours, while the co-pilot and the rest of the crew would go out to prepare the aircraft in a Walton dinghy supplied by the marine craft section.

Briefing usually lasted up to an hour and included information about the weather, communications, the latest intelligence reports of enemy shipping and aircraft, as well as pertinent information about the composition and last known position of the convoy. By the time the briefing was completed and the rest of the crew were aboard, more than three hours would have elapsed between the early call and the aircraft's finally becoming airborne. Add another three hours at the end of an eighteen-hour patrol and the crew would have been on duty for twenty-four hours. The next day was stand-down and was invariably spent sleeping until late in the day.

The third day the crew was on standby and could be sent off on another eighteen-hour patrol. In periods of intense activity it was not unusual for a crew to log 360 flying hours in a month.

Each convoy was designated by letters and numbers that indicated its destination, and was also given a code word to be used in the event it became necessary to break radio silence by using voice transmissions. This was only done as a last resort if the convoy could not be found, or had been scattered by persistent attacks by U-boat wolf packs. The NOT MET signal was sent by wireless transmission and was deliberately kept as brief as possible, for it could, if intercepted, betray the fact that the convoy had lost its air cover and was vulnerable to further attack. The last thing that any of our crews wanted to do was to put the merchant shipping and the escorts we were supposed to be protecting at further risk.

Late in March we were ordered to escort a convoy with the code name CHILD, which had left Halifax en route for Liverpool.

The convoy consisted of some eighty merchant vessels carrying food, munitions, and fuel, and had just passed the halfway point when it was harried by a pack of U-boats at a point several hundred miles southeast of Rockall, an infinitely tiny speck of rock in the mid-Atlantic. When we arrived at the last reported position there was no sign of the convoy and we started a square search, using twice the visibility distance between legs. The skipper ordered the NOT MET signal to be sent, together with our position.

An hour later we sighted part of the convoy and the single code word PREGNANT was sent, which signified 'I am with child.' The second half of the convoy was found an hour later and a further one word signal was sent: TWINS. All these precautions were employed not to be cute but to keep our transmissions as short as possible.

A spirit of friendly co-operation prevailed between the crews of Coastal Command and those of the Royal Navy. In order to keep our gunners in practice we had regular exercises with the Fleet Air Arm in the skies above Algeciras Bay or with submarines in the waters below. The Navy's Force 'H' was based at Gibraltar and included not only capital ships, like the Rodney and Renown, and the aircraft carrier Formidable, but submarines of the Thunderbolt Class.

Sometimes we would provide a slow moving target for the carrier's Grumman fighters in what was quaintly described as 'fighter affiliation.' This exercise would provide the opportunity for Fleet Air Arm pilots to make mock attacks on us, thankfully without using their guns, but recording their potential effectiveness with wing-mounted camera guns.

In a reversal of roles, the carrier would send up a Swordfish towing a drogue target for our gunners to fire at. Our problem was that we were not much faster than the target aircraft and had to wait until it passed within range before we could open fire. It was an embarrassment to our gunners when the tug aircraft dropped the drogue over our base so that we could see there were no perforations in the target.

Sometimes we would be invited to take a cruise in one of our submarines so that we could see sea warfare from the perspective of the hunted. It was a chilling sensation when the conning tower was emptied prior to diving and the main hatch clanged closed. It takes a certain kind of courage to be locked like a sardine in a can for days on end, but then they would say the same of our job when we took them up in a Catalina to view a mock attack on their own submarine. *Chacun a son gout!*

These official visits also led to some wonderful social exchanges. We were invited to the Formidable's Ward Room for pink gin and hors d'oeuvres and were delighted to share the only feminine company to be found on the Rock.

Some forty WREN officers and ratings were employed at Naval Headquarters and were invited to parties by all three services. I was invited to a reception to host some visiting entertainers at the residence of the Governor-General, Sir Mason MacFarlane, and it seemed as though most of the WRENs not on duty were present. On another occasion we were invited to a swimming party by the skipper of one of the RAF's Air Sea Rescue Launches. We were picked up at our own dock and ferried around to the east side of the Rock where there was a sandy beach, and where some WRENs had been invited to share a picnic lunch. They must have had a wonderful time during their period of duty at Gibraltar, but there was also the constant reminder of the hazards of war. They had to travel from the U.K. in one of the Navy's vessels and shared all the dangers of sailing in convoy. One detachment of WRENs was lost when the ship they were travelling in was torpedoed and sunk off the coast of Portugal. There were no survivors.

Early in April, Harry Sheardown's aircraft became due for a major inspection and engine change at the Scottish Aviation factory at Gourock on the banks of the Clyde. This was an opportunity for the crew to have a fortnight's leave while their aircraft was being serviced. Since our squadron was composed of Commonwealth personnel from Canada, Australia, or New Zealand, most of them made an immediate beeline for London, where they invariably stayed at the Regent Palace Hotel. Harry was anxious to meet up with his buddy, Johnny Johnson, another Canadian skipper, who had left Gibraltar about a week before us, and had left Harry a cryptic message: GOT PUT GOING UPSTAIRS. Harry roared with laughter, but I hadn't a clue what it meant until Harry explained that they had a bet on who was going to get into the pants of the charming young lift operator, and Johnny had beaten him to it.

When we returned from leave, I was transferred to a different crew, this time led by Brian Tait, an Australian, whose co-pilot, another Aussie, had left to take the captain's course at Killadeas after flying a total of 500 hours as second pilot. I looked forward to flying with Brian, who had a reputation as a fine flying boat captain, one from whom I could obviously learn much. I found Brian to be generous at sharing his knowledge and experience.

He went out of his way to teach me the finer points of landing and taking off in rough seas and would often allow me to make a landing at the end of a patrol, and to taxi the aircraft through the maze of shipping that was anchored between the alighting area and our mooring buoy. I wasn't aware of it then, but he was grooming me for the time when I would be ready to undertake the captains' course myself.

April and May were busy months for the squadron as the Allies were bringing the North African campaign to a successful conclusion and preparing for the assault on Sicily and Italy. My log book shows that I flew seventy-seven hours in April and 183 hours in May, bringing my total operational flying to 480 hours, more than enough to qualify me for the next step in my career. Accordingly, when Brian's aircraft was due for its scheduled overhaul in early June, and I accompanied the crew on the flight from Gibraltar to Plymouth, I knew it would be my last trip with 202 Squadron as a second pilot. Before I left the squadron I learned of my promotion to the rank of flying officer and also was awarded the 1939-43 star for operations I had flown at Gibraltar.

As we flew up the coast of Spain and Portugal, Brian went back into the cabin and I occupied the left-hand seat. We were carrying a VIP, a senior naval officer, back to England, where he held an important position on Admiral Max Horton's staff at Combined Headquarters in Liverpool. He was a career naval man, very knowledgeable, who had spent many years in command. He was able to identify all the lighthouses along the Iberian Peninsula, knew their individual characteristics, and the duration and frequency of their lights, all without reference to a chart. He was delightful company and had a great sense of humour.

We were flying over a lone British merchant vessel that was under the protective escort of a Royal Navy destroyer, when our flight engineer reported that anti-aircraft fire was bursting astern and at our height.

Without hesitation I fired off the recognition signal of the day, a two star red/green Very cartridge.

The naval officer chuckled and leaned across to yell at me: "Don't blame them for being trigger happy. They've probably been shat upon from a great height too many times to be caught napping. If they really wanted to hit you they could probably do so. You're a sitting duck as far as they're concerned."

Although I couldn't see the humour of the situation, believing that the Navy lookouts should be able to identify the distinctive outline of the Catalina, I could understand the attitude of the destroyer's skipper in wanting to make it patently clear that he didn't welcome the close proximity of any aircraft, friendly or not.

The remainder of the flight was without incident and we flew across the Eddystone Lighthouse on our way into Mount Batten. After landing in Plymouth Sound, we were met by an RAF pinnace that came rushing out to guide us into the safe anchorage within the breakwater, directing us to a mooring buoy inside the Cattewater, near the hangars of Number 10 (RAAF) Squadron who operated Short Sunderland flying boats.

Brian Tait was well known to his fellow countrymen of Number 10 Squadron and it was a happy throng that repaired to the bar after dinner. Brian introduced me to his mates as "that Pommy bastard who's going to make a great flying boat pilot one of these days." He knew that I would be celebrating my twentieth birthday in a fortnight and he wanted this Saturday night to be an occasion to be remembered and, as soon as he discovered that there was a big dance at a hotel on Union Street, he set about organising transport for us.

Despite my protestations that I didn't dance, I soon found myself taking the short ferry ride across the Cattewater to Sutton Harbour. A brief walk up through the Barbican and we were soon at St. Andrew's Church, or what was left of it after the Luftwaffe had had its way. It was a clear soft night and the sky was lit by a full June moon. For a wonder, there was no air raid and we walked the length of Union Street without a care in the world.

Brian led the way into the foyer, paid for two admissions, and strolled into the dance hall with his bushy red moustache bristling like radar antennas.

"Look over there, Robby. The strawberry blonde with up-swept hair standing next to the brunette by the band. Let's go over and introduce ourselves."

And with that he grabbed my arm and marched me over to where the two girls were smiling at us. He made a beeline for the brunette and as he swept her on to the dance floor he made vigorous gestures for me to do likewise.

The girl smiled at me encouragingly and I was gazing into her blue eyes fumbling for the right thing to say when she broke the awkward silence.

"Your Aussie friend isn't half the fast worker. They think all the Devon girls are attracted to their dark blue uniforms. We don't see many RAF pilots in Plymouth. I know you can't tell me where you're stationed, but you can't be from the Aussie squadron at Mount Batten. Are you on your way through?"

"Yes, I'm going off on two weeks leave, to my parents' place in London. Look, can I see you again? I mean when I'm on leave. I don't want to spend the whole time in London, and I was planning on a cycling tour through the West of England."

When she smiled a pair of dimples appeared on her cheeks and I noticed what a beautiful peaches and cream complexion she had.

"Whose the fast one now? Don't you think we should have one dance first, before you take me home? I think they're just about to play the last waltz."

I was immediately flooded with relief. The slow waltz was about the only dance I could manage without tripping over her feet. I took her in my arms as the band started to play "Who's taking you home tonight?" I looked across the dance floor and caught Brian's eye and he gave me the thumbs up.

It seemed only a short walk to Betty's home, but it was sufficiently far that I had time to decide I wanted to see more of her. I knew we would be leaving Plymouth early in the morning and that as soon as the aircraft had been delivered to Scottish Aviation I would be heading down to London on leave. When I was last at home, I had ordered a custom-built touring bicycle from a small shop on the New Kent Road, not far from the Elephant & Castle. I had told my parents that I planned to spend at least a week of my leave touring the West Country, and I now wanted to know how Betty felt about my spending some time with her in Plymouth. When I broached the subject she was quite excited at the prospect, but seemed to find it hard to believe that I would want to cycle down from London to see her. She was only eighteen, but had already seen three years of war and it was natural for her to be a little cautious about wartime romances and promises.

When we reached her doorstep, she turned up her face and as we kissed she whispered, "You will come down to see me soon?"

I told her that I couldn't wait to see her again and that it would be a matter of days before I would return. As I walked back to Mount Batten I was already thinking the thoughts of a young man in love. I was lucky that everything went as planned. We took off early on Sunday morning and before noon had landed on the River Clyde and handed over the aircraft to the Scottish Aviation representative at Gourock.

I bade a hasty farewell to the crew and promised to keep in touch with Brian, then caught the night train to Euston and arrived home in Streatham by nine o'clock on Monday morning. Dad was having a cup of tea with Grandma and I joined them at the breakfast table to catch up with the latest news. The previous Friday night a landmine had exploded over Streatham

Vale and had created much damage to roofs and windows. Our roof was covered with a tarpaulin and several of the windows were blacked out with tarpaper mounted on flimsy lath frames. Grandma seemed to have grown more nervous and tremulous and I wondered how many more sleepless nights she could take and whether she would survive another winter of relentless night raids. By the gentle way he spoke to his mother, I could tell that Dad had similar thoughts.

I told him of my plans, but didn't mention Betty by name, and he offered to come with me to pick up the new bike. We took the tram from Streatham Common, down Brixton Hill, past the Kennington Oval to the Elephant & Castle. A short walk down the New Kent Road brought us to the small bicycle shop nestled under a railway bridge. The bike was ready, a splendid ultra-light weight, beautifully crafted and finished, and modelled after the famed Claude Butler racing bike. Dad had to work the late shift and took a tram to book in at the Camberwell Green depot. As I rode proudly home, I marvelled at the smooth operation of the three-speed derailleur gears and of the contrast to the roadster on which I had delivered papers before the war.

There was hardly any traffic as I left home the following morning under a cloudless sky with the sun at my back, and pedalled down the high road toward Reading, I was wearing shorts, an open-necked shirt, and a rainproof windbreaker. I carried a small rucksack on my back with a change of clothes, and, slung from the back of the saddle, a rolled rain cape with a tire repair kit inside. As I rode steadily along, I revelled in the clean fresh smells of the countryside and watched the miles tick by on the miniature odometer attached to the front fork.

Sometime after noon I was enjoying a lunch in the garden of a pub on the outskirts of Chard in Somerset. The landlord brought out a glass of cider and a plate with thick slices of crusty bread, dairy butter, some cheddar cheese, and a dish of pickled onions. I seemed to be the only customer and he stopped to admire my bike and to chat. I told him I was enjoying a spot of leave and was headed for Plymouth and he asked me how long it would take me.

"I could make it by ten o'clock tonight, but I thought I'd break the trip and stop somewhere near Exeter. Don't want to push it too hard on the first day and my girlfriend isn't expecting me until tomorrow."

"Well, then," the landlord's ruddy face creased into a smile, "you've stopped at the right place. My widowed sister runs a decent little bed and breakfast just this side of Exeter Town. She used to charge two shillings for a comfortable bed and a fine West Country breakfast. If you tell her you stopped at the Three Choughs and had a spot of lunch with her brother Jack, she'll like as not be able to find you a bit o' supper. I can tell by your sun tan that you've just got back from foreign parts and you must be pretty fit to 'ave come all this way in one day. But you'll need to keep up your energy, young sir, if you'm goin' to court a Devon lass, you mark my words."

I was warmed by his kindly interest, thanked him for his suggestion and paid the bill, a grand total of sixpence. As I wheeled my bike up the path he called after me.

"Don't forget the name. Mrs. Mary Hinton. At the foot of the hill going into town. Number eight Railway Terrace. Tell 'er Jack sent you."

When I knocked on her door early that evening, I noted the trim little lawn, the neatly tended flower beds, and the carefully laid out herb garden. Mary Hinton opened the door and was pleasantly flustered when I mentioned that her brother Jack from Chard had recommended her bed and breakfast.

"Do you come in, zir," she blushed. "He does exaggerate, does our Jack. Always 'as and always will. But if I do say so myself, you'll get a good night's sleep 'ere and a fine breakfast to send you on your way. Now, I charges two shillings the night, but if you want supper I can do that too for two and six."

"That would be splendid, Mrs. Hinton. I'd like to have a bit of a clean up first, and I wonder if I can bring my bike 'round the back. It's brand new and I forgot to buy a lock and chain for the trip."

"Oh, don't you worry about that sort of thing. Nobody would dare touch your bicycle if it's in my front garden. But you'm welcome to wheel it 'round the back and put it into the potting shed—though I doubt we'll see rain tonight, or for a week to come. Now, I'll fetch you up a pitcher of hot water. By the time you'm washed supper will be on the table in the kitchen."

She showed me up to a front bedroom with a bay window and a beautiful view over the sleepy little town of Exeter. It was a large room with an enormous brass bed taking up most of the east wall space, an oak sea chest at the foot of the bed, and a wash stand in the bay window. I stood for a couple of minutes savouring the beauty of the Devon countryside and thinking of the Devon lass I'd be seeing tomorrow. I couldn't help thinking also of how peaceful rural England was, and of the contrast between the way these good country folk lived and the lives of those Londoners who, like my family, lived in dread of the uneven drone of enemy aircraft in the night sky, the whistle of falling bombs, the crump of anti-aircraft guns, and the heavy thump of exploding bombs. I thought also how lucky I was to be fighting over the waters of the North Atlantic and took comfort in knowing that at least I could count on returning to a comfortable bed at the end of each flight.

When I got down to the kitchen, Mrs. Hinton had laid out an inviting supper of cold pork pie, fresh garden salad, homemade chutney and, for dessert, a large bowl of trifle topped with thick Devonshire cream.

"Like as not you'm ready for a nice cup of tea with your supper." She placed a large tea pot between us and covered it with a bright floral tea cosy. "Now, I can tell by the way you talk that you're from up Lunnon way, but what brings you down to Devon?"

"I've got a couple of weeks leave and I'm going to Plymouth to see the girl I'm going to marry." Somehow, my relationship with Betty had progressed.

Mrs. Hinton was that self-sufficient sort of country woman who enjoyed nothing more than a good conversation because she kept up a steady stream of comments and questions, often without the need for me to do more than nod or smile whilst I was tucking into her delicious supper.

"Isn't it awful the way them Plymouth folk had to suffer those terrible hit-and-run raids? If you can believe all you read in the papers there's no place you can be safe, not even in an air-raid shelter. Still, we'm lucky they don't bother us much in Exeter, though we did have the sirens go the other day. After they'd dropped their bombs, of course! No one hurt, I hear, but a couple of cows had to be slaughtered up at Highfield Farm. Jim Gurney could only let me 'ave a pint o' milk the next morning, instead o' my usual quart. I do like to make a little clotted cream every day for tea time, makes the scones taste different with a spoonful o' my home-made strawberry jam. So you'm gettin' married to a Devon lass? Well, good luck to you both. Times is uncertain, Lord knows, but we must keep on going. Hitler's got another think coming if he thinks he can push us around. I reckon Mr. Churchill has told 'im off proper and he's right, too. We won't give up easily. We've stood up to the Spanish and the French, before my time, of course, and we won't knuckle under to the Germans."

There was much more of the same and I was content to listen to her chatter as she bustled about, bringing more food from the pantry and filling up my tea cup whenever it was empty. I must have been full and comfortably lulled by her voice, because I found myself getting sleepy. She noticed my eyes droop and was immediately apologetic and concerned.

"Look at me run on so. You must be tired out, poor lamb. Now you run along up to bed and I'll clear the table. If you want to sleep in that's quite all right. I know when my Tom comes home on leave, he doesn't want to be disturbed. Mum, he says, I have to get up early enough in the Army. When I'm home I like to lie abed on a Sunday. Doesn't get up 'til seven-thirty sometimes! Now, you just take your time and I'll bring you up a cup of tea and some hot water for your shave when you're ready."

I smiled to myself as I thought how different our biological clocks worked.

She considered rising at seven-thirty to be a luxury, probably because she had always been up by six, whereas for the past six months I had been following a routine when I could be eating breakfast at three in the morning and another breakfast at twelve o'clock the same night. But I was glad to be making an early night of it for I was anxious to be on the road again by eight.

I slept soundly and was awakened by the birds singing in the apple tree below my window. I dressed quietly, but Mrs. Hinton must have been listening for me because there soon came a tap on the door and in she came with a tray of tea and biscuits, together with a pitcher of hot water.

"Breakfast'll be ready when you are," she smiled. "You'll need a good start to the day if you'm cycling all the way to Plymouth. Can't keep your lass waiting for you, can we, me dear?

Despite the enormous supper I'd eaten, I was ready for breakfast. There were fresh brown eggs, cured bacon, fried tomatoes, crispy potato slices and a plateful of hot toast with farm butter and strawberry jam. When I had finished the meal, and was enjoying a last cup of tea, I asked Mrs. Hinton how much I owed her. She wouldn't accept a penny more than two shillings and sixpence, so I gave her a half-crown and thanked her for her kindness. She saw me to the gate and stood waving until I pedalled out on to the road.

I had told Betty that I would be arriving by noon on Tuesday, but the early start, together with the absence of motor traffic, saw me sailing down the hill and into Plympton just after eleven. Betty lived in the Astor Housing Estate at Mount Gold on the eastern edge of the city and although I took my time I was outside her door at a quarter to twelve. In my naivéte and excitement I had overlooked the niceties of arriving a little late rather than a few minutes too early. Of course, few houses had telephones in those days and I had no way of warning them of my early arrival. The result was that I knocked on the door and met Betty's mother for the first time, thoroughly flustering her by catching her with her hair still in curlers.

Mrs. Fahey left me standing at the front door and called upstairs to her daughter, who was still in the throes of finishing her own make-up, and then disappeared into the kitchen. Betty herself came tumbling downstairs and greeted me, blushing with a mixture of excitement and embarrassment.

"Mum, come and meet Alan. He's come all the way down from London. Isn't that exciting?" I could tell by the look on her face that Mrs. Fahey would have chosen a different word, but she emerged from the kitchen and shook my hand and invited me into her home. She led the way into the front room and immediately excused herself on the pretext of making tea. I was about to say something but was stopped by Betty's warm embrace and a long kiss on the lips. When we came up for air we were both very flushed.

When Betty's mother returned with the tea things, she had somewhat recovered her composure and set about supplying me with tea, Devonshire cream, jam, and scones (which she called 'tuffs'). The next hour or so was spent in learning a little more about each other's families. I found out that Mr. Fahey worked in some sort of clerical position in Plymouth Dockyard; her eldest brother, Bob, also worked there as a welder; her middle brother, Doug, was serving in the army somewhere in the Middle East; and her youngest brother, Ken, was still living at home and attending the local council school. Her father had served in the Great War, and had been a professional football player/coach in Oran. A family wedding photograph in sepia tone was produced, showing Mr. Fahey as a dashing young sergeant in uniform, together with a pretty young wife who might have been the twin to her eighteen-year-old daughter who sat next to me smiling with pride. Betty was working in a department store at Drake's Circus, had just been promoted to buyer, and was anxious to introduce me to some of her friends and to show me her favourite haunts in Plymouth. Mrs. Fahey sensed that we wanted to be on our own and hustled us out of the house with an admonition not to be late for supper.

"Betty, don't forget your father likes to have his supper on the table sharp at six, so try to be back by five-thirty at the latest, so you'll have time for him to meet your friend. Now, best bring your bike into the back garden, Alan, just to be on the safe side, and off you both go and enjoy yourselves."

We rode the bus from Beaumont Road to Drake's Circus and then walked down the Barbican to Plymouth Hoe. I cannot remember much of what we said, but I knew that I wanted to marry this smiling young woman with the twinkle of mischief in her eyes. It was evident, too, by the way she clung to my arm that she had eyes for nobody but me. I do remember wondering how I was going to be received by Mr. Fahey, but with the carefree optimism of youth I put my fears behind me and trusted that he would be putty in the hands of his wife and daughter. I also remember being continually filled with wonderment that a chance meeting that brought two people together in the middle of a war, could produce such immediate and strong emotions. But then, what did we know of life? I was just twenty and she was only eighteen.

We got back to Betty's home on the dot of five-thirty, just before her father arrived. Betty's twelve-year-old brother was suitably impressed by my bicycle and asked me how much it weighed, how fast did it go, and how much did it cost, until his mother interrupted his questions and sent him off to wash his hands before supper. Mr. Fahey came into the house and it was immediately evident that he was the archetypical Victorian patriarch. Everyone in the family was quick to respond to the needs of the breadwinner. Slippers were brought, an ashtray was positioned convenient to his favourite chair, and a fresh cup of tea placed at his elbow. He was immaculately dressed in blazer and flannels, with a crisp white shirt and starched collar, and a white carnation in his lapel. We sat sizing each other up, the old warrior and the young warrior, both prepared to accept each other for the sake of the girl we both loved. When he heard that I had been at Oran, his polite reserve disappeared and he spoke of the happy years he had spent with his wife and young family as the player/coach of that city's professional football team.

Soon our conversation widened to include the Allies' progress in the war and we exchanged respectful opinions of the respective strengths of our enemies and allies. The two women, mother and daughter, seemed to hold their breaths until it was evident that Mr. Fahey had accepted me as a *bona fide* suitor for the hand of his only daughter. Then the supper table became a relaxed place of celebration, with everyone joining in the conversation as Betty and her mother brought freshly-baked Devonshire pasties from the kitchen, fluffy white mashed potatoes, and vegetables fresh from the garden. By the time dessert was served all tensions had eased and I felt like one of the family, which was a good sign, since I hoped to become one of them in the very near future.

As if to confirm my impressions, it was tacitly accepted by everybody, including the youngest son, that I should spend my leave in their home and that I should occupy Doug's room, who was on active duty overseas and not expected home until the tide of battle had turned. Naturally, I couldn't be more delighted and looked forward to my all too short seven day's leave, and to spending as much time as possible with my new-found love.

It was as though everything in that June of 1943 conspired to make that one week's leave full of happiness. The weather was breathtakingly radiant. Each day dawned to bright sunlit skies with puffy little clouds of fair weather cumulus drifting in from the south-west. We took the Cremyll ferry to Cawsand and climbed up to Maker Heights where we spent a thoughtful half hour sitting in the old church that had stood since the time of William the Conqueror. Betty whispered that she would like to be married in a church like this and we started to make plans for an early wedding, as soon as I had completed the captains' course. We walked close together along the cliff walk to Rame Head and looked down into the empty space of Whitsands Bay where the gulls were sailplaning in the updrafts that rose from the expanse of white sand.

Another day we took the bus to Roxborough and walked into Yelverton for a lunch at the pub on the village green. It seemed that we couldn't have enough of togetherness and we talked of the future with hope and optimism, although we both knew that there was every likelihood that I would be sent overseas shortly after completing my course, and that there was a distinct possibility that the first year, even years, of our marriage would be spent apart. We both agreed, as we walked beside the stream that ran into the River Plym, that we wanted to take the immediate risk of being apart so long as we could be together in the future. We decided to talk to Betty's parents as soon as we got home, believing that they would understand the urgency of the way we both felt. Our evening meal was special for several reasons. It was my last day in Devon, and I had to return to London before reporting to my new posting. It was also my twentieth birthday and Betty's mother had prepared a special dinner to celebrate the occasion. We had both agreed that we would wait until the end of the meal before making our announcement, but as dinner progressed our nervousness became evident. I found myself talking more than usual while Betty's usually animated manner was replaced with a thoughtful quietness that finally prompted her mother to speak.

"You'm quite the Little Miss Sobersides, m'dear. What's the matter? Cat got your tongue?"

Two bright spots flushed on Betty's cheeks and she reached for my hand. "As a matter of fact, Mum and Dad, we have something to tell you." She took a deep breath. "We're going to get married."

Bill Fahey looked across at his wife and spoke in mock seriousness. "What did I tell you, my dear? I said we'd be hearing something like this the way these two young love birds have been behaving this week."

"Oh my, oh my! Are you sure, my dears? And you've only just turned eighteen, Betty. Are you really sure that's what you both want?" The expression on Mrs. Fahey's face was a mixture of concern and happiness.

By the time the meal was over we had their blessing and started our planning for the wedding. The next morning we walked up to St. Michael's Church, arranged for the banns to be read and booked a date with the vicar for the wedding service to be held on the sixteenth of October, subject to the exigencies of the service, as the minister stated with some practicality. Our next stop was a jeweller's at Drake's Circus where Betty picked out her engagement ring, thence to the department store so that she could share her joy with her friends at work. It was the day after my twentieth birthday.

I had decided to save time on my return to London by taking my bike on the train from Plymouth to Reading, leaving me with a short ride to Streatham, where I would spend the last night of my leave trying to explain to my family all that had happened in the last seven days. Their reaction was predictable. My sister Ruth was excited at the prospect of being a bridesmaid, my mother was sceptical, and my Dad was positive but neutral in his usual cautious and deliberate way.

1943: A Crew of My Own

I CAUGHT THE TRAIN to Liverpool and took the ferry from Heysham to Larne, just outside Belfast. From Belfast, the journey to Enniskillen, via Armagh, was serene and peaceful as the little Ulster railway line wound its slow way through the lush green countryside of Northern Ireland. Fortunately, there was a small dining car which served a decent luncheon that not only satisfied the inner man but also served to pass time on the journey to Enniskillen.

RAF Station, Killadeas, was a small flying boat base at the eastern end of Lough Erne, in a little cluster of islands which provided sheltered moorings from the prevailing south-westerly winds. The main alighting area was a long taxi to the west end of the lough, where three operational squadrons were based at Castle Archdale, and where I had landed on the trans-Atlantic flight from Gander. The headquarters of Number 131 (Coastal) Operational Training Unit consisted of a small group of Nissen huts (again) and a hangar situated on an expanse of concrete hardstanding with a launching ramp. Our quarters were some distance away on the main road to Enniskillen at St. Angelo, a single runway airfield built by the Americans. Even at the end of June, the weather was overcast and the wind that blew in from the Atlantic was heavily laden with moisture that produced a climate of almost incessant rain showers and low stratus cloud. It was next to impossible to keep clothes dry and the sheets and blankets on our beds felt damp to the touch.

The hut that I was assigned to was similar to the ones that I had lived in as an airman, except that these were divided into two large rooms, with four beds in each unit. It was fairly spartan accommodation, but adequate to our needs and certainly bearable for the time that we would be on the course, a period of three months or so, depending on the weather, and the serviceability of the aircraft. Each unit was equipped with a potbellied stove, but there was a shortage of fuel, and we could only have a fire for a few hours each evening after suppertime, and we usually turned in early to keep warm.

When I arrived, two of the four beds were already taken. I dropped my travel bag on an empty bed and introduced myself to the sole occupant, a tall grey-eyed Australian who wore the half-wing of a navigator on his dark blue battle-dress blouse.

"I'm Dick Bayliss, from Melbourne," he announced. "I'm your navigator, and our other cobber is Don Plastow, from London. He's our second dickey and he's just stepped out for a shave in the ablution hut. I've just got in from Bournemouth. Only been in the country a week. Was on a troop ship for three weeks before that. Came around the Cape. Spent a couple of days at Durban. Bonzer place, that was. Sunny and warm. Is this what you jokers call summer? Seems more like winter to me."

Before I had time to answer, the door burst open and a slim figure wearing a pilot officer's greatcoat slammed the door behind him. He sat on his bed and hugged his coat around him, his thin body shivering and his pale face frowning with displeasure.

"What a bloody country," he said. "No wonder they wear

141

the green on St. Patrick's Day, the whole bloody country's going mildew with the damp. Let's hope we get posted to somewhere warm at the end of this course. That is if we survive. You must be our new skipper. Don Plastow, your second pilot. Just finished AFU on Oxfords at Cranwell." He held out his hand.

As I shook his hand I was conscious of weighing them both up, of forming first impressions. I'd learned the habit when I was a young cadet in the OTC, and had found it to be a useful way of assessing a person's character. Not that it was infallible, nor that it was incapable of being modified, but simply that it was an early warning of potential areas of conflict or misunderstanding.

My impression of Dick was that he was sure of himself, confident of his ability to perform his job, the sort who would back you up if he were sure you were right. At the same time, I sensed an inner intensity of spirit, and a readiness to smile that gave promise of a good sense of humour. I later found that he was deeply religious, a non-smoker, and a teetotaller. Not exactly your tough Aussie from the outback, but I was wary of jumping to conclusions.

Don, on the other hand, was a little more difficult to fathom. He appeared at first to be a bit of a whiner, and the pallor of his skin indicated that he could possibly be a liability if the going got really rough. Yes, it was cold and damp in the hut, but nothing that we couldn't cope with. Despite his bold manner of speech, he appeared to be physically frail, nervous and uncertain of himself. Of the two, it seemed that Dick would make a better deputy and I decided to keep an eye on my second pilot and to delegate responsibility to him only when he had demonstrated his fitness. I needed someone I could rely upon in an emergency, someone whose judgement I could count on.

Six newly-formed crews assembled at nine o'clock the following morning in the Nissen hut that served the dual purpose of briefing room and intelligence library. There were fifty-four officers and senior NCOs weighing each other up and trying to gauge the experience and qualities that each man would bring to the task that lay ahead.

Our first experience in common was to report by crews to the photo section to have our crew photos taken. Looking at that picture almost sixty years later reminds me of how young we were and how grimly we faced the camera. I had already met the second pilot and the navigator. Now I could put a name and a face to the other members of my first crew, all of them sergeants.

Frank Sleigh, the flight engineer, who had gone through the apprentice school at Halton, was a qualified engine fitter and deliberate of speech. When we first met he had saluted and smiled confidently. I was to learn later how dependable his judgement could be and how knowledgable he was about the reliability of the two Pratt & Whitney Twin Wasp aero-engines that would have to carry us all over thousands of miles of sea and across several oceans.

Another Aussie on our crew was Sgt. Mick Tunney who hailed from Perth. He looked to be about no more than eighteen and masked his immaturity with a cocky attitude that reminded me a little of Mickey Rooney in the film "Boys' Town." He was our rigger, or fitter airframe, and he would prove to be invaluable as our expert in mooring up to a buoy, or in anchoring in shallow waters. He also achieved the distinction of falling off the bow and being hauled aboard at the blisters, in fresh water or sea, more times than any other rigger in the squadron.

Ron Smith was one of two wireless operator/air gunners (WAGs), and stood over six feet tall, which was a decided disadvantage in the cramped forward cabin, which he shared with the navigator and the radar operator. He had a dry wit, and, although he rarely broke into a smile, had a great sense of humour. He also turned out to be a remarkably fine air gunner and a good all-round crew member.

Sgt. Hodgson was our wireless operator mechanic (WOM), a small wiry man, who seemed at first to be a little shy and lacking in confidence. As we got to know each other, I found him to be invaluable at keeping the radio and radar sets tweaked to give their best performance, no easy matter when you remember that wireless telephony was still rather a hit and miss affair. The various components were rack-mounted in the forward cabin and took up a great deal of space. Their efficiency depended to a large extent on the operator's flair for trouble shooting and for knowing how to get the best range and signal strength from the wireless valves (tubes). Jack was the kind of operator who always seemed to carry the right selection of spare valves.

Our second engines man was Jock McDougall, from Glasgow. Like many Scots, he was taciturn of speech, but had a quick smile and a ready joke when things were not going well. He and Frank made a good team, and both served as back-up cooks when our rigger needed extra help in the galley.

The other WAG was Sgt. Holding, a tall, dark man, who bore an amazing resemblance to my father, though he was only a

couple of years older than me. He was respectful, addressed me as Skipper, and was the type who withheld judgement, although I got the distinct impression that he was sizing me up. Later, I came to count on his steadiness under pressure and depended on his stable influence on the rest of the crew.

Our first flight together was scheduled for that afternoon, and we were accompanied by Flight Lieutenant Inglis, the flight commander, who gave me an introduction to the local flying area. He sat in the second pilot's seat and watched the crew on our first departure from the mooring buoy. Once both engines were idling steadily I signalled Mick to drop the short slip that held us to the buoy and made a slow turn into the passage between the islands that led to the main lough. As we neared the pinnace that served as our air traffic control, the flight commander obtained clearance for take-off and I lined up the aircraft into wind and carried out the final check before opening the throttles. The steady wind from the west and the light chop on the surface created ideal conditions for the first take-off with my new crew, and as we climbed steadily to circuit height I felt I had passed the first test.

"You'll have to keep an eye on Church Hill to the south," Inglis indicated a range of hills over to port. "There's no problem in daylight, but keep in mind it's there. One of 423's Sunderlands piled in there on it's return from patrol last month. No survivors. Circuit height here is normally 1,000 feet so as soon as you level off you can start a turn on to the downwind leg. The island you can see to starboard is Boa Island and just off shore is our low level bombing range. You can see the target buoy marked with silver radar reflectors. I'll shut up now and leave you to concentrate on the landing. Try to touch down right by the control boat, but make it a touch and go."

A touch and go landing is what the name implies, the aircraft is not allowed to come to a complete stop, but while it is still riding on the step, take-off power is applied and another take-off and landing is made. After the third circuit had been successfully completed, Inglis indicated that I should allow the aircraft to complete a normal landing run and taxi back between the islands to our mooring at the east end of the lough, pointing out the red (port) and green (starboard) buoys that marked the passage.

"Remember 'right red returning,' and keep the red lights to starboard at night, green lights to port. You follow the rules of the sea when you're on the water, same as any surface vessel. If you meet other traffic, use your horn to indicate your intentions. One blast means 'I am turning to port,' two blasts 'I am turning to starboard,' three 'I am going astern,' four 'the way is off my ship,' and five is a general distress signal, quicker than SOS and more easily recognised by mariners."

As we approached the 'trots,' the mooring area, Inglis indicated which of the several vacant buoys he wanted me to use. He chose one in the row closest to the shore, which meant I would have to manoevre the Catalina between two other moored aircraft, leaving me with an awkward exit path if we failed to pick up the buoy. In the still backwaters I could tell that even with the engines idling we would have too much forward way (speed) for Mick to have adequate time to bend down and slip the free end of the heavy hawser through the loop on the top of the buoy and secure it by taking a couple of turns around the mooring post on the port side of the front turret.

"Rigger, stand by for mooring. Blisters, stand by to deploy drogues. Engineer, stand by to stop engines." I waited until we were as close to heading into wind as the crowded space would allow, and kept the buoy in sight just to port of the bow. "Drop both drogues together. Be ready to trip drogues for a missed approach."

The Catalina slowed as both drogues provided the necessary drag. I added a touch of power to ease us up to the buoy, and felt the tenseness go out of my body as Mick deftly ran the short strop through the loop and took a double turn around the bollard. He turned and gave me the thumbs up sign and I switched the 'SECURE' signal to the 'ON' position, duplicated in Frank's position, to show him that I had no further need of the engines. As the flying boat swung safely at its moorings, I turned the ignition switches off and looked across at the flight commander, waiting for further instructions.

"As soon as the main mooring pendant is made fast, I want everyone ashore and in the briefing room for about half an hour." We felt a light bump as the dinghy arrived to ferry us ashore. "You come ashore with me, Skipper, and we'll send the dinghy back for the rest of the crew."

I followed him aft to the blisters, passing Dick, who had had little to do on our first trip but look out of the blisters. "Nice going, Skipper," he whispered, and gave me a wink.

In the dinghy, Inglis took out an oilskin tobacco pouch and began loading an old briar pipe. When it was packed to his satisfaction, he cupped his hands around a box of Swan Vestas to shield the match flame from the breeze, and, when his pipe was drawing smoothly, flipped the spent match into the water.

"Looks like you've got a good crew there, Robby. They all seem as keen as mustard not to let you down, and they were anticipating your commands. I noticed that your navigator, Bayliss, had the drogue lines untangled and ready to cast overboard before you gave the order. He had his helmet on and was plugged into the intercom listening to your instructions. What you need to do now is to get to know them as individuals. Find out what their strengths are, what they are interested in. I like the clear way in which you give orders. No room for misunderstandings when you're in a tight corner. But don't be too impersonal. You've proved to them that you are fit to command, and they will already have judged you by the three smooth landings you pulled off. Don't forget that things won't always go so right for you. Oh, and by the way, I'd let your rigger know that you'd like him to clip his safety belt to the hull when he's mooring up. The water will be a lot rougher when the wind freshens and you don't want to lose him overboard."

I passed on these words of wisdom to Mick, but he shrugged his shoulders and told me that the belt restrained him from bending low. I could see his point, for the ledge he stood on was three feet above the waterline, and often he would only have a few seconds opportunity to pick up the buoy. It was the first of many decisions I would have to make that required the captain to allow each crew member a certain amount of individual leeway in the way he carried out his job. The best I could do with Mick in this case was to urge him not to take unnecessary risks, but it took him a long time to learn the lesson and several dunkings in cold water before he found the right solution. But he was a skilled rigger and, after a time, he used his ingenuity and with the help of a sewing palm he lengthened the restraining straps on his safety belt, thus enabling him to reach closer to the mooring buoy.

And what of the skipper himself? I realised at the time that I was a young skipper and lucky to be given the chance to command my own crew so soon after my twentieth birthday, but I had already gained in confidence from my service in the OTC, the Auxiliary Fire Service, and from the excellent flying instruction I had received with the U.S. Navy. Nevertheless, the reality soon dawned on me that my crew, skilled as they were in their respective trades, ultimately depended on my decisions in all aspects of operating a flying boat wherever we might be sent in the world. It was comforting that the flight commander had gained the impression that the crew cheerfully accepted me as their leader, but I was also painfully aware that things had gone well up to now, and that my abilities as captain had yet to be tested. I knew more than any of us how much had to be learned in the brief ten weeks that comprised our operational flying training. We were at the beginning of what was to be a concentrated period of flying exercises that were designed to develop the individual skills of our crew. Our first test came with our introduction to night flying. My own experience as pilot was limited to a couple of hours in the clear summer nights of Pensacola and the painfully few hours that could be squeezed into our advanced flying training in the overcast skies of southern Gloucestershire. I realised that I had flown less than 700 hours as pilot-in-charge. Nearly sixty years later the number of night take-offs and landings I had accomplished seems woefully inadequate, but I suppose if we thought about it at all we simply did what was expected of us.

The first night, we left the moorings at Killadeas and taxied our way through the waterways between our base and the main alighting area in Lough Erne. A strong breeze was blowing from the west, driving the rain-soaked clouds from the Atlantic and creating a stiff chop, sending showers of spray into the propellers, which in their turn sent swirls of water to mix with the sheets of rain that lashed the surface of the lough. Our instructor, Flight Lieutenant Hulme, sat in the left-hand seat and I took the co-pilot's seat whilst Don stood on the catwalk between us in order to see the red and green buoys that marked the channel. As we emerged into the main lough, Hulme pointed out the flarepath, which consisted of half a dozen small dinghies, each equipped with a small mast carrying a white light, the individual craft being joined to the next by a hundred yards of towline, and the whole flotilla being towed behind a power boat occupied by the duty air traffic controller.

This luckless officer was responsible for keeping the flarepath in line with the surface wind and acted a as general director of the traffic in the circuit which could amount to half a dozen aircraft at any one time, there being one Catalina and two Sunderland flying boat squadrons operating from Castle Archdale at the western end of the lough.

To assist the Duty Air Traffic Control Officer in keeping track of incoming and outgoing traffic he was equipped with the rather primitive radio telephone system that was installed in our aircraft. Under ideal conditions it had a range of about ten miles, but in practice we found it rarely reached seven miles and for long range communications we relied on wireless transmissions or visual signals in Morse code using an Aldis signalling lamp. For controlling the traffic that was involved in carrying out night take-offs and landings—more commonly referred to as 'circuits and bumps,' the Aldis lamp was the preferred method. An aircraft wishing to take off or land would flash its call letter in Morse and the DATCO would flash the same letter in red or green. As a last resort DATCO would fire a single red or green star from his Very pistol, always a dramatic reply.

When we were ready for take-off, Hulme nodded for me to flash our call sign and we were answered by a green. He lined up with the lights of the flarepath and opened both throttles to full. My hand closed below his and he nodded again as he turned his attention to the flying controls. With our light load and the stiff breeze to help us we were soon airborne and climbing to the west as the mass of Church Hill loomed menacingly on our port beam.

"There is a right circuit in effect when the wind is westerly," Hulme said as we climbed away. "That will keep us clear of the high ground to port. Remember that Church Hill is 1,200 feet above sea level and the standard circuit height is 1,000 feet. If the cloud base is below 1,000, you'll have to fly the circuit just below the cloud base. Don't forget, the weather has a nasty habit of deteriorating without warning. You'll get lots of practice at low altitude circuits at this place, but if the visibility is reduced to a quarter of a mile and the ceiling drops below 500 feet, don't waste any time, but land immediately. It's not healthy to be swanning about these hills at night."

The aircraft reached circuit height and Hulme reduced power until we were cruising at a comfortable ninety-five knots, then banked the Catalina in a steady turn until we were flying on the downwind leg.

"I'm going to show you the technique for landing at night. Wait until the first flare disappears under the wing, count five, throttle back and begin a 180 degree turn that will take you to the final approach. Align yourself with the flarepath, increase power and trim the elevators until your speed is seventy-five knots and your rate of descent is 200 feet a minute. Maintain that attitude until you feel the keel touch the water, then throttle back and haul the yoke into your chest until she rides down off the step."

Hulme was an excellent flying instructor and an above average flying boat pilot. He demonstrated a copy-book night landing whilst keeping up a steady patter of instruction. Within fifteen minutes I had completed three moderately successful power landings and was on the final approach for the fourth when a red Very light soared up from the flarepath. I obediently poured on climbing power and went around for another attempt. This time I had turned late on the final approach and the flarepath seemed a lot further away than usual so I maintained an altitude of 500 feet until I thought it safe to descend.

"Well done, Skipper," Hulme said. "I was wondering if you were going to land short. Not a good idea to lose sight of the flarepath. Some of these small islands rise to 300 feet and you don't want to bump into one of those small hills. Let's make three more landings and call it a night."

But we had hardly alighted on the main lough when the DATCO called us up on the R/T and announced that night flying was cancelled and all aircraft were ordered to return to base.

"Funny, doesn't seem to be anything wrong with the weather. Wonder what's up? Take it easy as you taxi back through the channel and have the second pilot check off the marker buoys as we navigate through the islands. You might make a practice of having a couple of the crew stand watch for other aircraft or surface vessels approaching from your stern."

I sent Sergeants Smith and Holding back to the waist blister positions and warned them to keep a good look out. As we passed between the last two islands before reaching the trots, Smith drew my attention to some activity on the larger one.

"There's a lot of lights moving about, Skipper. Not near the shoreline, but up in the trees. Can you see, sir?"

Hulme picked up his microphone before I had time to respond. "Thank you, blisters, we'll find out what it's all about when we get ashore. But right now I want everyone to assist the skipper as we prepare to moor up. Let's have the second pilot take my seat so he can stand by with the signal lamp."

With that he exchanged places with Don Plastow, who opened the roof hatch and stood on the seat with the Aldis lamp at the ready. His lamp picked up our mooring and we were soon safely riding at our buoy. A dinghy was waiting to take us ashore and as we rode back the coxswain told us the story of the lights Sergeant Smith had seen. An aircraft had crashed into a hillside on the approach to landing. One pilot was dead and there were several serious injuries. The dead pilot was one of my classmates at Pensacola. His death was the thirtieth since our class of ninety-three cadets had started training together a little more than eighteen months previously. It was a sobering introduction to the hazards that would face our crew in the years ahead.

The following weeks were packed with a series of exercises that were designed to test the skills of every individual as well as our ability as a crew to work as a cohesive team. Our gunners were given an opportunity to use live ammunition against both airborne and surface targets. A flight of Miles Magisters was based at the small airfield of St. Angelo just east of our base and they would be briefed to rendezvous with us over Donegal Bay where they would stream a drogue which our waist and front turret guns would attempt to hit. Our top speed at level flight was a bare 112 knots and I had the utmost difficulty in keeping pace with the target plane. Except for Mick, our rigger, who was the only one to hit the target drogue, our boys made up with enthusiasm what they might have lacked in expertise, but they all fared better on the surface target, an aluminium sea marker which we dropped in the sea. The radar operators used a small reflector target on Innishmurray Rock to practice homing the aircraft in on simulated night or bad weather attacks, and all airgunners gained valuable practice in tuning the bulky radio receivers and in sending and receiving wireless transmissions in Morse code.

Don Plastow, my co-pilot, was given much opportunity to fly the aircraft, and to practice landings from the left-hand seat, something that I had not been given the opportunity to experience when I was a second pilot at Gibraltar.

He also earned himself the Most Highly and Derogatory Order of the Irremovable Digit for Perseverance in Bombing a Moving Target.

The Patron Saint of this award was one Pilot Officer Prune, who was a fictitious character appearing in the Royal Air Force Training Manual (TM), where he served as a horrible example to erring pilots in various instances of poor airmanship, such as landing with the wheels up. Don's award arose from an incident when we were carrying out low-level bombing practice on a marker buoy in Lough Erne. The target was about a quarter of a mile off shore near Boa Island, where the road from the Republic of Eire linked the island to the mainland by a small wooden bridge.

Over the bridge on this particular morning rode an unsuspecting postman delivering the daily mail. We carried twelve eleven-pound practice bombs, which were supposed to be dropped in pairs to simulate the first and last in a stick of six depth charges. As we approached the target, Don's role was to ensure that the correct number of bombs was selected, and that the distributor arm was cocked and set. I was concentrating on the target and at the optimum point I pressed the bomb release button. I didn't notice that Don continued to reset the wiper arm as my thumb firmly pressed the bomb release.

As a result, we dropped not two but six bombs, the last pair neatly straddling the bridge, causing the startled postman to fall off his bike. As we banked low over Irish territory we were treated to the spectacle of a civil servant of a neutral power being assaulted in the reasonable discharge of his duties. Luckily for us this potential international incident never came to the attention of the higher powers.

Dick's prowess as a Coastal Command navigator was not tested until near the end of the course, when we were sent off on three operational flight exercises out into the Atlantic, two by day and one by night. For all intents and purposes these were standard general reconnaissance patrols and were treated as such by giving us all the opportunity to shake down as a crew, and were preceded by a thorough briefing and followed by a detailed debriefing. We were given such information as call signs, colours of the day, the position and location of friendly forces, as well as the last known position of enemy U-boats and the whereabouts of enemy aircraft patrols.

My impressions of Dick's navigational skills had already been partly formed by his skill at mapreading, the appearance of his navigation logs (which were a model of neatness), and the meticulous plotting of his charts. However, where he really impressed was in the cool, unhurried way he went about his business of keeping track of our dead reckoning position, plotting our drift, and by his superb technique of checking and cross-checking his work. On a long flight, he would be the only member of the crew to get no relief, and it was both encouraging and assuring to see how well he performed, even in the foulest of weathers. It was odd that he could be so confident of our position when we were flying through a North Atlantic cold front, where the visibility was abysmal and the cloud base only 300 feet above the surface, whilst I was up front, worrying whether we were flying an accurate course and speed. The accuracy of his navigation was only as good as the accuracy of our flying.

We finished the course at the beginning of October and the whole crew celebrated by going to Enniskillen for a meal of steak, eggs and chips, washed down by drafts of thick Irish porter. The next day we were aboard the train for Belfast where we were transferred to an RAF bus for the short ride to Newtownards, where we were to spend the next week on a fitness and survival program, culminating in a mad dash over a commando obstacle course. Some of the crew grumbled at the prospect of foot slogging, but when we were pitted against another Coastal Command crew, they rose to the occasion, and excelled themselves, our gunners out-performing the rest of us with their accuracy at firing the Sten gun. I had been introduced to the Sten gun when I was going through recruit training, but I could never achieve a consistent standard of accuracy, although I had been good enough to represent the OTC. at Bisley.

At the end of the course we were sent on two week's embarkation leave, and were issued with travel warrants to Number 302 Operational Ferry Unit, which was based at Oban, in Scotland. We caught the night ferry from Larne to Stranraer and said our goodbyes at Glasgow, where we boarded trains for various parts of England. Dick and I travelled to London with Don, then Dick and I caught the Cornish Riviera for Plymouth. I was to be married on the sixteenth of October and Dick was accompanying me to Plymouth where he would stand up for me as my best man.

From the moment I stepped off the train at North Road station and fell into the arms of my bride-to-be the clocks seemed to be moving at double time. The family had been on tenterhooks lest my leave should be delayed or cancelled altogether. The banns had been read the required three times; bridesmaids' dresses, made from materials bought with precious clothing coupons, had been delivered, returned for alterations and redelivered. My mother and sister were arriving from London the next day, and my father was due to arrive a day later.

The ceremony itself was typical of wartime weddings: the groom and best man in dress uniform; many of the guests, both men and women, wearing uniforms of one of the three services; the old church decorated with blossoms from the gardens of friends and neighbours. And, of course, the eighteen-year-young bride looking radiant in her white wedding gown.The wedding reception was held at a large old hotel on Plymouth Hoe and was a jolly family affair. The day passed in much of a blur, but at last we were on the Southern Railway train from Priory Station and on our way to a brief honeymoon in a lovely old cottage on the Sussex Downs with a magnificent view of the English Channel.

A taxi took us from Chichester to the tiny village of Mid Lavant, and we lugged our suitcases over a stile and hiked up to the top of the hill where Aunt Jane lived in splendid isolation. She welcomed us with open arms and spoiled us with delicious meals which she cooked over an open fire. The cottage had no electricity or running water, but we were oblivious to these minor inconveniences. We enjoyed the romance of dining by the light of oil lamps, going up to bed by candle light, and drawing sweet, fresh water from Aunt Jane's well. For the next week we were waited upon, free to rise or sleep in, remote from the war that lay just across the channel, and, unlike people in large cities like Plymouth and London, relatively free from attacks by enemy aircraft. We roamed the downs and returned to Aunt Jane's country cooking, and to the seclusion of her cottage snuggled in a wood on top of the hill. The only person we saw apart from Aunt Jane was a Canadian Army dispatch rider who stopped by to check his position on the map. Aunt Jane welcomed him in and plied him with tea and fresh scones baked on a griddle over the hearth, and I gave him a pipeful of my favourite tobacco.

All too soon it was over and I took my new bride home to Plymouth, where we said our goodbyes with the sure knowledge that we would soon be separated by thousands of miles, for many months, possibly years.

THIRTEEN

First Command

OBAN IS A SMALL HARBOUR on the west coast of Scotland at the head of the Firth of Lorn and to the east of the Island of Mull. It is protected from the weather that sweeps in from the Atlantic by the small island of Kerrera and is a safe haven for flying boat operations except when the winds blow from the southwest, particularly during the months of January and February.

While we were on the ferry training course, we were accommodated at the Loyola Hotel, a residential hotel built in the reign of Queen Victoria. It was a cold and cheerless building with plumbing that was, for its time, the very latest in Victorian design and technology. The flush toilet had its idiosyncracies and would only operate according to a set procedure: one firm tug on the chain, a three second pause, a second firm yank, and a quick release of the chain. The inscription on the bowl was "Symplicitas," but we were firmly of the opinion that it would be more appropriately named "Complicaticus," for it never worked first time for anyone but our navigator. Only Dick, apparently, had the right mechanical bent.

I took over my first command, a Catalina, serial number FP 252, on January 14, 1944. For the next four weeks my efforts were focussed on the task of preparing myself and my crew for the 8,000 mile flight to India. Now I was no longer the student captain, learning the ropes under the tutelage of more experienced pilots. Now the onus was upon me to make every decision, no matter how important or how trivial, that concerned the safety of the crew and the success of our mission. No longer would I be comforted by the thought that my every action would be supervised by a more senior pilot, who was duly authorised as the aircraft captain. I was now that duly authorised person and, no matter how inadequate I might feel about my readiness to assume the burden of that authority, it was mine and mine alone.

Our training area from mid-January to mid-March was a 2,500 square mile expanse of sea between the Inner and Outer Hebrides, bounded by the Islands of Skye and Mull in the east to the islands of South Uist and Barra to the west. The weather at this time of the year is familiar to those who have sailed the North Atlantic and for the most part consists of low stratus cloud, poor visibility, and steady rain, the consequence of a seemingly endless series of cyclones that track over the Western Isles. Several of the islands boast mountain peaks that are higher than 2,000 feet and there is no room for errors of navigation. The majority of our flights involved flying at or below the cloud base, which generally meant that we were flying at from 300 to 500 feet above the water, depending upon the uncertain effectiveness of our primitive radar system and the visual alertness of every member of the crew. Even with six pairs of keen eyes on visual watch and the skill of our radar operator's interpretation of the small cathode ray screen, we had some close calls. Once, when we were returning from a night navigational exercise, I decided to take a shortcut to avoid deteriorating weather and the likelihood of gale force winds by entering the narrow passage between Morvern and the Isle of Mull. The channel, called the Sound of Mull, is barely two miles wide and about ten miles from Tobermory to Oban. Halfway through the channel, a combination of lowering cloud and driving rain forced us to fly at fifty feet above the water. I breathed a great sigh of relief when the front gunner spotted the flashing light that marks Duart Point and points the way to the sheltered waters of Oban's harbour.

Between January 16 and 24 a series of storms made it impossible to fly at all, and I was ordered to maintain a gale watch in case the aircraft broke its moorings and was driven ashore. I divided the crew into two watches and took the first watch myself, with Jock, the second flight engineer, Ron Smith, the wireless operator, and Mick Tunney, the rigger/gunner. The second watch I put in command of Dick Bayliss, our navigator, with Don, the co-pilot, Frank, the first engineer, and the two wireless operator air-gunners.

The small marine craft that carried us out to our flying boat made heavy going of the rising seas and the dinghy operator had great difficulty in approaching the port blister to put us aboard. The wind and the seas were causing the tailplane to swing through a vertical arc that threatened to smash the small boat and as soon as the four of us were safely aboard we waved the coxswain away. Although the aircraft were moored in the lee of the island of Kerrera, the gusty winds were causing our Catalina's anchor cable to snatch at the buoy, each time sending a shudder through the hull and threatening to carry away our mooring pendant. I decided to start the engines with the aim of keeping enough power on to take the strain off the mooring and to keep us on station and at the same time keeping the aircraft pointing into wind. I couldn't tell how long we would have to keep this up, but I knew we had enough fuel to keep the engines idling for forty-eight hours. And I knew we had enough food and emergency rations to last several days. Fortunately we were able to ride out the storm after spending two uncomfortable nights aboard, and it was with great relief that we welcomed the arrival of a dinghy to take us ashore.

After the gale had spent itself, the weather entered another phase and we were prevented from flying by several days of thick sea fog and low stratus clouds. Knowing that FP252 was going to be our own aircraft for the foreseeable future, the whole crew took pride in scouring it clean from stem to stern. The bilges were pumped dry, the duck boards lifted, and every scrap of detritus was collected and removed. The rigger inspected all the canvas on the mainplane and tail surfaces and applied patches where necessary, then polished all the plexiglass blisters and hatches to provide clear visibility for the watchkeepers. The flight engineers gave our auxiliary power unit a thorough overhaul, knowing that its readiness to start up might be crucial to the safety of us all. Dick, our navigator, devised special stowage places for his charts and navigation equipment, not so much to define his territorial space in the main cabin as to produce an orderly working environment.

For my part I held rehearsals of all emergency procedures so that the whole crew would be prepared for any eventuality. Our experience with the gale watch had taught us that we should expect the unexpected and to be ready for the worst. I had read the Coastal Command Intelligence Summaries that analysed aircraft losses and learned that troubles rarely occur singly, and that small incidents have a habit of escalating into major problems that can culminate in disaster unless dealt with promptly and with conviction. What we lacked in experience as a crew, I was determined to make up for by forward planning and regular crew training.

One thing I had learned from my general reconnaissance course, and from the time I had spent patrolling the wide expanse of the Atlantic Ocean as a second pilot, was the need to impress upon every crew member the absolute necessity of keeping a vigilant visual watch. For the most part we would be flying in marginal weather conditions in poor visibility seeking a target that was almost impossible to detect with the rather limited and primitive radar equipment at our disposal. Radar works on the principal of a sender/receiver device which emits radio waves that are bounced off a target and returned to the originating instrument where both range and bearing can be calculated and displayed upon a cathode ray tube, in essence a small television screen. The problem we faced in flying over the ocean was that the troubled surface of the sea itself presented our radar with a series of targets as each wave rose and fell. These individual waves sent a return signal which showed up on the radar screen as "grass" or "mush," which effectively masked the targets we urgently needed to identify, a U-boat or its periscope.

Accordingly, I made every navigation exercise into a simulated active search. There were seven watch positions to be shared by our crew of nine, and since the duties of the navigator and the wireless operator kept them confined in the main cabin, every other crew member was assigned a sector of sea and sky as his particular responsibility for maintaining a visual watch: the front gunner covered a sector forty-five degrees on either side of the bow, the two pilots covered their respective sectors from the beam to forty-five degrees to port and starboard respectively, the gunners in the blisters watched from the wing tips to the tail plane on each side, and as a bonus the flight engineer kept watch from his position under the wing on both sides of the aircraft. I reminded the crew that the Coastal Command Intelligence Summary gave our chances of sighting the enemy about one for every 1,000 hours flown. In 1943, a normal tour of operations in Coastal Command was 1,000 hours and took nearly a year to achieve. Thus, our best hope for a sighting could only be achieved by our vigilance and alertness throughout the period of our flights, usually of eighteen hours' duration.

My aim of achieving this high standard of watch-keeping was tempered by the need to prepare us all for the long voyage to India. Such a flight placed a tremendous responsibility upon the navigator and both pilots, as well as upon the rest of the crew. And we had a scant two weeks to complete our training programme.

Finally, we all had to be inoculated for yellow fever, bubonic plague, and typhus, since we would be flying through areas of the world where these diseases were prevalent. We had forty-eight hours to recover from these uncomfortable jabs before we took our aircraft up for its final air test before leaving Oban. Prior to our departure I was handed my orders: "Flying Officer Robertson and crew are to proceed with Catalina FP 252 to 240 Squadron, Madras, and are not, repeat NOT, to return to the United Kingdom."

FOURTEEN

Bound for India

ON FEBRUARY SEVENTEENTH 1944, we took off at first light from the lee of Kerrera Island and looked back at Oban for the last time. Our route took us down the west coast of Scotland, Wales, and England and after five hours we landed at Plymouth just after noon, where we refuelled for our next leg to Gibraltar. I was painfully aware that my new bride was only a short distance away across the Cattewater, but I had no means of contacting her, and, in any event, I had far too much to occupy my time before we slipped out of Plymouth Sound just after dusk for the long night flight to Gibraltar.

We had been briefed to fly south along the ten degree west line of longitude in order to keep well clear of the coast of occupied France, and out of the range of marauding Junkers 88's that roved from their bases in France out over the Bay of Biscay. As soon as we had cleared the English Channel I gave orders to test fire our machine guns, a sober reminder to all the crew that we were now entering enemy airspace. I was glad that we had the cover of darkness and rather enjoyed flying along just below broken stratus cloud at about 1,000 feet above the sea. Both of our Pratt & Whitney radial engines were synchronised and gave off a harmonious and reassuring steady drone, and our flying instruments gave me nothing but comforting information.

All was as it should be until the door to the navigation compartment was opened by a worried-faced Dick.

"Something's wrong, Skipper. Are you sure you're steering 155 degrees?"

"That's what I'm showing on my compass. What's the problem?"

"Well, either we have a stronger easterly wind component than I was expecting, or there's something crook with our compass. Alter course sixty degrees to port and I'll take a drift reading. When I've got a fix, I'll give you a new heading for Cape St. Vincent."

My feeling of well being was shattered and I started to think back over our preparations for the trip. Had I hurried Dick over the crucial compass swing before we left Oban? Was there something inherently wrong with our flying that had produced this problem so early in our journey? It suddenly dawned on me that I was ultimately and solely responsible for the safety of this aircraft and its crew, a realisation that was reinforced with every mile of our journey.

Fortunately, the sun broke through the cloud as we were rounding the tip of Southern Spain, and we were able to check our position with radio bearings and visual landmarks from Cape St. Vincent through to the Straits of Gibraltar. As we approached the familiar waters of Algeciras Bay, I concentrated on the business of assessing the water surface in the alighting area and planning the best direction for the landing run. The Air Traffic Control pinnace flashed us a green and I brought the aircraft into wind and across the gentle swell. One slight skip and we were safely down.

A dinghy from the Marine Craft Section came out to greet us and signalled us to follow it into the familiar mooring area between the main runway and our quarters at East Camp. I recognised the coxswain as he slowed to point out our mooring buoy and to request permission to come alongside our port blister. It felt like coming home after a long absence, although it was only nine months since I had left Gibraltar to start the Captains' Course. I waved him in to the blister and picked up my flight bag before leaving the cockpit.

"Don, you stay with the crew and secure our mooring pendant. Dick, grab your navigation gear and come ashore with me. I want to arrange for us to do another compass swing as soon as possible. We'll send the dinghy back for you, Don. You'll all need to bring your overnight kit, and don't forget to bring mine and Dick's bags."

The coxswain gently slid the clutch into astern and backed carefully away from FP252. As we went ahead and cleared the port float I looked back at our aircraft as it sat bobbing gently in the calm waters of Algeciras Bay. I was determined to get to the bottom of our navigational problems and hoped that 202 Squadron's Navigation Leader would be able to give us a hand. Moose, a Canadian from Claresholm, Alberta, was much respected by the aircrews and was a hardworking and generous officer. I already had a respect for Dick's approach to his job, but I was aware, as was he, that he lacked experience. I wanted to be sure we could rely on our compass on the long leg to Cairo.

Fortunately for us, Moose was in his office at Squadron Headquarters, and greeted me like a long lost friend. As I introduced him to Dick, I sensed that the two of them would not only be able to speak to each other as specialists, but that they would hit it off as colleagues and friends. Moose listened carefully as Dick related the steps we had taken on our compass swing at Oban and knit his eyebrows into a slight frown as he concentrated his thoughts. At last he spoke.

"Most of the ferry aircraft that come through here have seen at least two years of operational service. Some, like FP 252, have been around longer, and have undergone several refits and modification of equipment such as radar and armament. This has meant that the deviation errors affecting the compass have changed drastically and it's simply not good enough to do an air swing. We've sent signals back to Oban recommending that all aircraft do a ground compass swing, but we know the pressures that they're under to get these reinforcement aircraft and crews out to the Far East. I'm afraid there's nothing for it but for us to spend most of tomorrow with the aircraft hauled out of the water and towed to the concrete apron where we have sufficient room to check your compass where there is no interference with the aircraft's magnetic field. The delay can't be helped, but I'd sooner you took your time and got it right now, than have you plagued with problems over the remainder of your route. This next leg has to be flown at night and it's going to take you at least eighteen hours over mainly desert country."

I nodded in agreement and watched Dick's serious expression. I knew that he needed my help and reassurance.

"Moose is right, Dick. Much better to correct this trouble early or we'll never be really sure whether it's your navigation, my flying, or the damned compass. I'll give you a hand tomorrow, and we'll let the crew have the day off to explore Gibraltar. They've all been working hard over the past six months and they deserve a break. Don, too, he looks as though he would benefit from a little rest and recreation."

"Too right, Skipper. I'll get the swing organised with Moose and I'll see you later in the Mess."

Before leaving the Headquarters Building I stopped by to pay my respects to my former CO, Wing Commander Brian Dobb. His handsome dark face broke into a smile and he tugged at his luxurious black moustache. He turned to the other occupant of his office, Squadron Leader Armitstead, my former flight commander, and chided him gently.

"You see what happens when you recommend these young

boys for training as flying boat captains? Before you know it they'll be after our jobs and we'll be put out to pasture. What mischief are you up to now, young Robby, and how can we help you on your way?"

I explained the nature of our problem and told him that Moose had already suggested we do a ground swing in the morning, and that we'd probably be on our way the next day.

"Anything you want, dear boy. Nothing too good for former squadron members. Drop by the bar before dinner tonight and I'll buy you a drink."

I thanked him, but privately promised myself that I'd excuse myself as soon as I'd had the obligatory drink. I knew the reputation my old squadron had for their mess parties with the inevitable singsongs and solo recitals by senior members.

I recalled a wild celebration on the occasion of the twenty-fifth anniversary of the founding of the Royal Air Force, when I, a very junior second pilot, had been rescued by my skipper, Brian Tait, when I was in the process of lecturing our revered flight commander 'Bismark' Briggs on the nature of human temperament. At the tender age of nineteen and at two-thirty in the morning, I was in no fit state to instruct anybody on any subject, and I remembered that one of the least pleasant aspects of recovering from a hangover was the experience of sitting in the blisters looking down at the grey-green seas as they rolled and heaved below. On that occasion we had been unexpectedly called out on a search for a U-boat in the vicinity of the Salvage Islands, a search which had kept us in the air for nineteen hours.

To my surprise, when we arrived at the dock the following morning, we were greeted by Frank and Mick, the flight engineer and the rigger. They had chosen not to go into Gibraltar with the rest of the crew, but had decided that we'd need their assistance with the compass swing. I should have thought of it myself, because we had to arrange for a dinghy to tow us from our mooring buoy into the inner harbour where a beaching crew was waiting to haul us up the ramp and out to the end of the concrete apron. Whenever a flying boat is being towed by a marine craft, a qualified pilot and flight engineer must be on board in case the towline is lost and the engines have to be started. In that event, the rigger would also be required to handle the warping lines, and Mick had guessed correctly that his presence was required. After my initial feeling of guilt for not having thought this out myself, I was glad to see that the crew was coming together as a team capable of thinking for itself.

The procedure for swinging the compass was time-consuming and tedious. The aircraft had to be aligned with the compass rose painted on the concrete, and readings had to be taken on the magnetic compass on each of the main quadrants: north, east, south and west. Then the procedure was repeated all over again for the intermediate points: northeast, southeast, southwest and northwest. Even with the assistance of the beaching crew and a skilful tractor driver, it took us until noon to complete the swing. Fortunately for us a NAAFI wagon came out and we decided that there was no time for us to return to the mess for lunch, but settled for coffee and sandwiches.

During the break, Moose and Dick calculated the compass deviation and made the necessary adjustments to the compass. By the time they were finished and we had been towed back to our mooring it was five o'clock, too late for us to complete an air test and be ready for a take-off at dusk. Although I was impatient to continue our flight, I knew it would be imprudent to rush our departure for Cairo.

I arranged for the crew to meet on the dock at nine o'clock the following morning for the air test and as soon as the preliminary starting check had been completed I called the engineer to start the port engine. I heard him give the priming pump five strokes, then waited for the sound of the inertia starter to rise to a level hum, the starter to engage, and the propeller to turn.

Nothing happened.

"Port starter not meshing, Skipper. Something's wrong with the gear."

"How long will it take to check?"

"At least a couple of hours, Skipper. We'll try turning the propeller over by hand. If that fails, we'll have to rig the maintenance platforms before we can remove the nacelle cover. I'll need some help unstowing the stands, but we'll be as quick as we can."

I chafed at the thought of losing another day, but realised that nothing was to be gained by impatience and settled down to await Frank's inspection report. It was past noon before he came down into the cockpit and I could see by his face that it was not good news.

"The solenoid is not engaging and the whole starter unit will have to be replaced. By the time we get a maintenance crew out with a spare it'll be another hour or so. I doubt we can carry out an air test before dark. Sorry, Skipper."

"It's okay. It's not your fault, Frank. We'll just have to postpone take-off for another day. I'll call the air traffic controller and get him to send us out a dinghy. We'll plan to carry out the air test first thing in the morning."

As we waited for the dinghy to take us ashore, I thought about Moose's remarks about the age of our aircraft and wondered what further problems might be ahead. We had only covered 1,000 miles of our journey and had another 7,000 miles to go over unfriendly territory and rough terrain. Maintenance and refuelling facilities were few and far between, all the more so because we were a flying boat and must always find sheltered waters on which to alight. I knew from the list of emergency alighting areas that there were probably only a couple of places between Gibraltar and Cairo which could provide us with refuelling facilities.

The next day everything went smoothly. The air test revealed no further snags and Dick was guardedly cautious about the serviceability of our compass so I arranged for a crew briefing for 15:00 hours. I wanted the whole crew to be present at this important briefing which would not only include the weather picture and the details of the route, but also would contain information about enemy aircraft and shipping we might encounter en route.

As Moose had predicted, our flying time from Gibraltar to Cairo was estimated at nineteen hours and ten minutes, based on a steady following wind. We were routed inland from Oran to Sfax, across the North African desert which had been the scene of early battles between Mussolini's Italian Army and the British Eighth Army, thence to Tripoli and El Agheila, more recently the site of desperate armoured conflict between Rommel's Army and General Montgomery and his beloved Desert Rats. From there our route would take us across the Libyan Plateau to Cairo, where we would be landing on the River Nile at Rod-el-Farag, a former staging post of British Imperial Airways.

I decided to take off two hours before last light so that we would have the advantage of flying in visual contact for the landfall at Oran, partly for the comfort of flying with the setting sun behind us, and partly to give Dick as much opportunity as possible to check his navigation (and our compass) with as many visual landmarks as possible.

Leaving Gibraltar, we set course for Ceuta on the North African shore, then turned on to the easterly course for Oran. In light of our recent experience with our compass, I concentrated on steering an accurate course, checking frequently with our gyro compass and with the standby liquid compass.

Just as we had identified the lights of Oran ahead, Dick opened the cockpit door and passed up a new course for the long haul to Sfax.

"Compass seems to be okay, Skipper, and we're making

good ground speed. I'll need to take some three-drift wind sights every hour, but it looks as though the met. forecast is right on as far as wind speed and direction go. Our ETA at Sfax is 01:39 GMT, which is about 2:30 a.m. local time. Not much chance of mapreading until daylight when we're past Tripoli and over the Bay of Sirte. Flying for maximum range gives us a true airspeed of only 100 knots. It's going to be a long night, Skipper."

We were flying at 4,500 feet, but the recognisable smells of North Africa rose to our height, an indefinable mixture of sand, heat, smoke of dung fires, sweat and dust, and something besides that was undefinable but suggested all kinds of tropical diseases. As these thoughts passed through my mind, Don returned to the cockpit from his fourth visit to the chemical toilet at the rear of the aircraft. His pale skin looked even more washed out in the light of the blue fluorescent cockpit lights. He didn't look well.

"Sorry, Skipper. I'm having these terrible stomach pains, and I can't stop going to the toilet."

I guessed that he'd picked up a germ when he'd gone ashore at Gibraltar, probably from something he'd eaten. The same thing had happened to me when I first arrived at Gibraltar and I knew how uncomfortable it could be. The only way to reduce the pain was to lie down and keep warm.

"You'd better go aft, cover yourself with a blanket, and lie down on one of the bunks. That way you'll be near the can and will be able to get some rest. Try to sleep. I can manage here for the next few hours. Send Mick up to sit in your seat. Don't worry, we'll manage all right."

I settled comfortably into my seat and thanked my lucky stars that I felt fit.

We were flying above a layer of broken cumulus cloud and seemed to be suspended in space without any apparent movement. The Twin Wasp engines set at cruising power gave off a reassuring steady throb. If I leaned my head against the sliding hatch of my port window and rested my earphone against the plexiglass, this steady throb became a tingling sensation that travelled through my whole body and made me one with the aircraft. I felt myself getting drowsy and hastily moved away from contact with the window. Mustn't be seduced by the comforting vibration. Another seventeen hours to go before I can relax.

The door behind me opened and Dick stuck his head into the cockpit.

"Mind if I come up front for a couple of star sights, Skipper?"

I gave him the thumbs up sign and motioned to the rigger to slide out of the seat to make room for Dick. Mick nodded and crawled forward to the bow position. Dick brought his bubble sextant to bear on Polaris, normally a faint star but apparently clear enough to see in the black night sky above us. The sextant had a clockwork mechanism that averaged out the movement of the aircraft to give a more accurate reading of the star's altitude. Within a couple of minutes Dick had plotted the position line on his chart and handed me a message slip containing our revised ETA at Sfax. I switched on my intercom and called Mick, who was still lying in the bomb-aimer's position.

"How about a meal now, Mick? It's about time for supper and we might as well eat while things are quiet. Anything good in the rations?"

"Right, Skipper. We've got some fresh eggs, canned bacon, stewed tomatoes and soya link sausages. I can do some fried bread if you fancy some. I'll get Frank to pass you up a mug of coffee from the thermos. Just to keep you going."

Soon the tantalising smell of cooking wafted forward into the cockpit and I could picture the busy scene as Mick and Frank worked over the twin electric stoves in the cramped space of the centre compartment. Rations for the nine members of the flight crew were brought aboard in a couple of wooden crates and consisted of a mixture of fresh and canned goods. Apart from the time that we had been on gale watch at Oban, our two cooks had had very little experience at preparing meals in flight. Fortunately the night air was remarkably still and they had no turbulence to contend with. I hadn't realised how hungry I was until the door opened and a large enamel plate loaded with scrambled eggs, fried bread, bacon, and tomatoes was placed on my lap. The meal was hot, appetizing, and I was ready for it. The aircraft was flying steadily on autopilot, there was just enough glow from the cockpit lights for me to see the food, and my taste buds were chortling with joy. I thought of Don in the throes of Gyppy Tummy and hoped that his condition would not be passed on to other members of the crew.

About an hour after I had finished my meal, Don reappeared briefly in his seat, but then had to leave the cockpit because of spasms of stomach pain. I made a mental note to talk to the medical officer in Cairo to see whether we could carry some medication in case of similar inflight emergencies in the future.

Shortly before our estimated arrival time at Sfax, Dick passed up another position report, together with an amended ETA, showing that we were about fifteen minutes behind schedule. From the worried look on his face I could tell that something was puzzling him and his voice confirmed his fears.

"Navigator to Skipper, I've not been able to get a good reading of the wind speed at this altitude, but I think there's something odd happening with the forecast wind speed and direction. We should be crossing the coast line at Sfax now, but the radar shows us to be about twenty-five miles away from the coastline. I don't think it's anything to do with the compass, but I'll keep watching it."

"Pilot to Nav. As soon as you've worked out our ground speed for this leg, let me know. Flight Engineer, what is our fuel consumption?"

"Engineer to Pilot, we're burning seventy gallons an hour. We started off with full tanks at 1,760 gallons, and have 1,150 gallons left. We used up quite a bit of fuel in the long taxi out from the harbour at Gib. That gives us a little better than sixteen hours at our best range speed."

I did some quick mental calculations and figured that we would make it to Cairo with a ten per cent reserve.

"How long until dawn, Navigator?"

"First light is 04:59 GMT. We should get a clear pinpoint as we fly over Tripoli. Looks to me as though our forecast for twenty knot tailwinds over the whole route is a bit crook. My last drift sight and the star sights show us as having a beam wind of about ten knots. I'll have a better idea of our ground speed by the time we reach the Libyan coast."

I pulled my route map and the list of emergency alighting areas out of my navigation bag. The only suitable alighting area was on the Gulf of Bunbah, about seventy-five miles along the coast west of Tobruk. It seemed like the most likely refuelling spot, preferable to Tobruk itself, where the harbour was full of sunken ships from repeated raids by first the Italians and Germans, then later by the British. In any event, that would still leave us with a four hour flight to Cairo. But at least we had an option if the winds continued to adversely affect our ground speed.

By the time we reached Tripoli it was evident that we were experiencing strong head winds, and after further consultation with Frank regarding our fuel consumption I decided, to make the decision to land early at Bunbah and take on enough fuel to see us safely to Cairo. The proposed track from Tripoli to Bunbah crossed the Libyan coast again just to the north of Benghazi, and carried us over an ocean route which gave me a better feeling of security. I wrote out a signal to notify the ferry unit at Cairo that we would be late arriving and asked for the latest information on refuelling facilities at Bunbah. The answer that came back within the hour was not reassuring. The facility at Bunbah was closed and the alighting area had silted over and was no longer safe for landing. Cairo's advice was to land in the open sea outside Tobruk harbour and to request guidance from the Harbourmaster.

This was not particularly welcome news. I had no experience of landing on open waters, yet there was no alternative. We had to land short of Cairo, and we needed fuel. Although I knew that Don was still feeling weak, I knew I would need him up front for the landing. Better to get him up now so that we could go over the landing procedure together. He resumed his seat with a brave front, but had obviously been drained of all energy. To take his mind off his stomach cramps I left him at the controls while I went back to talk to Dick and the rest of the crew. I would need their combined efforts for this landing, and I was anxious not to spend longer at Tobruk than I had to.

There was scarcely room in the forward cabin for eight of us, but I needed everyone to understand the situation. I had no idea what mooring facilities would be available to us, and I knew the harbour at Tobruk to be congested with naval traffic and sunken ships.

"We're going to need an extra special lookout both during the approach to the alighting area, and later when we get inside the harbour. Jock, you'll be helping Mick up front; I'll need you in the tower seat, Frank, to operate the engine and float controls; I want one wireless operator on the set, the other two in the blisters to handle the drogues. And make sure the colours of the day are loaded in the Very pistol. We may not be expected. Everyone keep plugged in to the intercom and don't hesitate to speak up if you see anything that might lead us into trouble. Dick, I want you standing by up front to help me in case Don has another bad spell. Everyone, be prepared to act on signals from the alarm horn. Now, I'd better get back up front to relieve Don."

We approached Tobruk from the landward side and I flew a

cautious circuit over the town before heading out to the harbour mouth. The sea conditions were favourable: a slight rolling swell coming across the Mediterranean from the northwest, coupled with a light breeze blowing from the northeast. I chose to make my approach into the wind and along the swell line, using enough power to give a rate of descent of 200 feet a minute. As we neared the sea I could see that we would touch down along the crest of a long swell. The keel touched the wave, I pulled back the remaining power, and the hull skipped once, twice, then settled down in a flurry of spray. First task done, we're down in one piece. Now to find our way into the harbour and locate the mooring area.

"Starboard blister here. There's an RAF air sea rescue boat coming out to meet us, Skipper. He's flashing a message. FOLLOW ME. WILL LEAD YOU TO THE REFUELLING BUOY."

I poured power to the port engine and swung around to starboard and followed the speeding launch. As we entered the harbour mouth a naval tug began towing the anti-submarine boom across our wake to close the entrance. Our RAF guide launch passed us on to a slow-moving Royal Navy landing craft and shot off with a flourish of self-importance and a big bow wave.

"Better open your hatch, Don. Stand up on your seat with the Aldis lamp."

I was not at all sure of the intentions of whoever was in charge of the landing craft, but I didn't like the way one of its crew was swinging a lead-weighted line in our direction and circled away from him to starboard.

"Blisters here, Skipper. You're getting close to this large buoy to starboard."

I looked across the cockpit and saw the danger too late. In vain I gave the starboard engine a quick burst of power, only to feel a shudder run through the hull as the starboard float smashed into a large can buoy that must have measured twelve feet across.

"Stop engines. Bow position make ready to receive towing line."

All we could do now was to sit and wait for the towline and hope that the coxswain of the landing craft would not inflict any further damage. I sat and wondered what I could have done to avoid this collision. Should I have cut engines and let the Navy tow us into safe mooring? How much damage had I done to the float, and would we be able to fly the aircraft on to Cairo? How long would it take us to refuel? The answer to all of these questions would only be forthcoming once we had safely moored up, and we had the chance to more closely inspect the damaged float. Meantime, pointless to worry about what I should have done, better to concentrate on the job of mooring the aircraft safely to the refuelling buoy.

The first priority was to arrange the refuelling which proved to be more of a task than usual. There was no refuelling scow available and the only way of getting fuel up to the wing tanks was by means of a hand-operated wobble pump screwed into the lid of forty-four gallon drums carried in the landing craft. Unless a quicker way could be found we'd be refuelling until after dark.

I sent our navigator over to the landing craft to find out if there were other alternatives, and Dick must have exercised all his Aussie charm because someone remembered a gasoline powered pump, part of the equipment of a captured Italian flying boat that was moored nearby. Within the hour the Italian pump had been found, powered up and was soon happily pumping aviation spirit into our main tanks.

As soon as Frank was satisfied that fuelling was being performed safely and efficiently, he accompanied me on an inspection of the damaged float. We borrowed an inflatable dinghy from the Navy and paddled out to the starboard wing tip. The nose of the float was crumpled, but the aluminium skin did not appear to be broken and the float had not lost its buoyancy.

"Looks okay to me, Skipper. Of course we won't know if it will retract until we get into the air. I'll use the crank handle and wind it up by hand until we're sure that the retraction mounting is not distorted. Don't want to do further damage if we can help it, do we?"

Neither by his words nor his tone had Frank implied any criticism of my actions that had led to the collision. A problem had arisen. It had to be solved. All energies had to be concentrated on completing our assignment.

"Well, it's too late to make it to Cairo before dark, and as soon as we've finished refuelling we'd better get ashore and organise a meal and billets for the crew. A night's sleep will do us all good and we can get an early start in the morning. I'll arrange for a boat to pick us up at 08:00 hours, ready for a nine o'clock departure. I'd like to be landing on the Nile no later than one o'clock so that we can get the maintenance people aboard to check the damage to the float. Let's hope they have plenty of spares."

The accommodation at Tobruk was spartan, but adequate. It had been a long day, we were tired and hungry, and we were all glad to find that there was plenty of water for showers. The transit mess provided us with a nourishing meal of beef stew and a refreshing dessert of canned fruit and local fresh dates. I also took the opportunity to get some relief for our luckless second pilot, who was still suffering uncomfortably with diarrhea. The army medical officer prescribed a course of chalk and opium and by the next morning Don was able to return to duty, albeit a little more pale and gaunt.

The following morning we slipped our mooring and followed the pilot boat that was standing by to guide us out to the harbour entrance. Once past the boom I turned the aircraft into offshore wind and took off to the north. I banked gently to port and circled over Tobruk while Frank cranked up the floats by hand. We were relieved to find that the locks engaged and the aircraft behaved normally. Dick gave me the heading for Rod-el-Farag and confidently predicted an ETA of 13:00 hours. I handed Don the controls and consulted the route map and details of the alighting area. Naturally, we were restricted to one of two landing directions since the Nile River runs roughly north and south at Cairo. The approach from south to north was over a rail bridge leading to a reach of the river that ran straight for about a mile and a half, plenty of room for Imperial Airway's Empire Class flying boats, and obviously plenty of room for us.

It was with some relief that we left the great expanse of the Qattara Depression behind us and sighted ahead the fertile delta of the Nile and the unmistakeable outlines of the pyramids of Giza rising out of the heat haze. I could see that our track would bring us right over the railway bridge and switched on the Floats Down light on the yoke. By the time we were turning over the river the floats were safely down and locked and I concentrated on making a textbook approach. There was no wind and the surface of the river was broken by the wake from a small pinnace that was sent out to direct us to the moorings. We touched down gently by a line of houseboats moored along the east bank and followed the launch to our assigned buoy. This time, the coxswain kept well clear of the aircraft until we were safely moored and our engines were shut down. Only when the propellers had stopped turning did the boat come alongside our port blister.

A cheery, sun-tanned flight lieutenant came aboard and introduced himself as the officer in charge of the local maintenance unit. He took a look at the damaged starboard float and was quick to reassure us.

"We have plenty of spare floats here. Last week we had a Cat arrive from Malta with a holed hull. Didn't quite clear the harbour wall on take-off and had to run up on the beach just across the river. He won't be moving for a long time so we can take his starboard float. We'll have you off in a week."

Despite his reassuring tone, as we rode in the dinghy toward the shore I had some lingering misgivings, and thought again of Moose's words at Gibraltar about the problems that plague an aircraft, and the demands that are placed on the engines and airframe as it weathers the demands of operational flying.

I was also concerned that we were dependent on the good will and efficiency of the maintenance unit and its internal priorities. A week sounded like an awfully long time to be waiting in Cairo for a float to be replaced, yet, as the maintenance officer had implied, there were other aircraft ahead of us with various degrees of mechanical problems.

After a pleasant meal on the Imperial Airways houseboat, we boarded a bus for the transit quarters at Heliopolis. The adjutant at 216 Group Headquarters gave us a cheery welcome and assigned us to our billets, the NCOs to the Sergeant's Mess, and the officers to a block of spartan apartments just opposite the streetcar terminal. I shared a room with Dick and Don on the third floor, and we joined other ferry crews for meals and drinks in a bar and dining room in the basement. One of the old hands, a pilot who had just delivered a Hurricane fighter from Takoradi, had flown across the continent to Chad and up the Nile Valley to Cairo West airport. He introduced us to the barman and ordered a round of the preferred drink of ferry pilots, equal parts of Cherry Heering and Bols Avocaat. After a couple of rounds our plight began to feel less desperate and we began to look forward to exploring Cairo.

The next morning, the three of us walked across to the headquarters building and drew an advance of pay in the local currency, Egyptian pounds, referred to by the local troops as 'akkers.' We also arranged to visit the stores at Kasr-el-Nil Barracks so that we could make up the deficiencies in our tropical uniform issue. But first we wanted to return to the aircraft to find out how long the repairs would take. We reached the aircraft to find a leathery- skinned warrant officer standing on the main plane and examining the wing surface with an expression of distaste.

"You see these ripples in the skin, sir? That means you've got some distortion in the main spar. Unsafe to fly this aircraft until the mainplane has been removed and we've checked for further damage. Looks like you'll be here for quite a while."

My optimism of the previous evening evaporated as I struggled to deal with the implications of this new information. I had orders to deliver FP252 to Madras, and was specifically instructed not to return to the United Kingdom. We were a reinforcement crew and were supposed to take our place as a replacement crew in 240 Squadron.

I went ashore to tackle the officer we'd spoken to on our arrival. His response was to downplay the seriousness of his warrant officer's diagnosis. He had the same rosy outlook that he'd displayed the day before.

"Look, old chap, I'm sure it's not as bad as the wo thinks. I promised we'd get you on your way within a week and we'll do our best to fix you up. In any event, we're not equipped to tackle that size of job here. If you have to have the mainplane removed you'll have to fly up to the maintenance unit at Kasferit on the Bitter Lakes."

I pointed out that his warrant officer was of the opinion that our aircraft was unsafe to fly, but that didn't seem to affect his optimism.

"I'm sure the WO is worrying unnecessarily. It's only eighty miles from here to Kasferit. You'll be all right, you'll see. Now, we'll see about getting your float replaced, and you enjoy a couple of days taking in the sights of Cairo. There's a great belly dancer performing at the Diana Theatre, I'm told. Take advantage of the occasion for a spot of leave. You never know when you'll get another chance to see Cairo. Don't worry, I'll get word to you as soon as the float's repaired."

The shuttle bus dropped us off at Shepherd's Hotel, where we found a table on the terrace, ordered drinks, and sat watching the world of wartime Cairo pass in review. Now that the Allies had driven the enemy out of North Africa, life in Cairo had returned to its pleasure-seeking normality. There were apparently few shortages and the civilian population exhibited an attitude of carefree belief in the certainty of tomorrow's bringing better times, typified by the Arabic expression *mahleesh,* meaning not to worry, an attitude that was both seductive and insidious, as well as easy to apply to one's own circumstances.

However, we only had a couple of days to relish the delights that Cairo had to offer, and divided our time between swimming in the pool at the Heliopolis Sporting Club, or consuming mountainous ice cream confections at Groppi's restaurant on Sharia Soloman Pasha. We returned to our quarters at the end of our third day in Cairo to find a message awaiting us that the new float was in place and the aircraft was ready to fly to Kasferit.

The next morning we lifted off the Nile and flew sedately past the pyramids and headed east toward the Suez Canal. In under an hour we were circling the alighting area on the Bitter Lakes where battleships of the Italian Navy had been sitting since their surrender two years previously. A beaching crew had us moved up the ramp and on to the concrete apron, where an inspection crew was to take over as soon as we had left the aircraft. A one-ton lorry was waiting to take us to the transit quarters, and we were soon enjoying lunch served by Italian prisoners of war wearing starched white mess jackets.

After lunch, we returned to hear the bad news. The spar was bent and had to be repaired before we could continue. It would take six weeks. Kasferit had no quarters that could accommodate us for an extended stay, so we were forced to travel back to Cairo in the same one-ton lorry that had taken us to lunch. It was a tight squeeze for nine of us and our kit under the canvas canopy in the back of the vehicle, and it was a long dusty ride, with a surprisingly civilised break for mugs of hot tea at a NAAFI tent located in the middle of the desert, halfway between the Suez Canal and Cairo. It was a disconsolate crew that arrived back at Heliopolis long after the sun had gone down. It seemed that with the end of the day our hopes for resuming our onward journey had faded.

No matter how we tried to put a brave face on things, each day we spent in Cairo was tedious. To the administration we were a nuisance. We had to be accommodated, fed, paid, and, when necessary, given medical attention. Don surprised us all by displaying a patience and fortitude that was uncharacteristic. He revealed an interest in photography and contrived a diffusion enlarger out of scraps of wood, cardboard and cloth, making extension bellows from scratch using only a pen-knife, and picking up a convex lens for a few piastres in the local bazaar. With the acquisition of chemicals and developing trays, he was soon producing good quality enlargements from our small format box cameras. With this same ingenuity, he got us all interested in his hobby and we began to develop our own photographic skills. For me it was a salutory lesson in the resilience of human nature.

The day finally came when we were ordered to report to the airfield near Heliopolis for the short hop to Kasferit in an old Douglas Dakota carrying spares to the maintenance unit. There was plenty of room for our kit and we settled in to our canvas sling seats for the noisy, dusty flight to the Canal. When we arrived, it was proposed that we carry out an air test and, if all was well, to proceed to Lake Habbaniya in Iraq and thence to Bahrein, a small island sheikdom in the Persian Gulf. There we would refuel and after an overnight stop we would set out on the long leg to Karachi.

Although we had no intention of staying any longer at Lake Habbaniya than it took to refuel, misfortune conspired once more to delay us and we were forced to stay overnight while Mick Tunney did some running repairs on the fabric covering of the rudder and tailplane. He had been watching from the blisters and had noticed a tear, first in the trailing edge of the rudder control surface attached to the vertical stabiliser, then later in the upper surface of the elevator control. It took the better part of the afternoon for him to effect the repair, then he had to give the surfaces a coat of dope to tighten the fabric. By the time he was finished the sun was sinking and we secured the aircraft and went ashore.

The following morning we were airborne early for the short hop to Bahrein and I looked forward to a quick refuelling stop. Again fate intervened in the form of an outbreak of smallpox and we were placed under quarantine for an uncomfortable forty-eight hours. The temperature was 110° Farenheit with 100 percent humidity. The transient accommodation consisted of a row of bamboo huts on the beach constructed with open lattice walls designed to direct the sea breezes to ventilate the sleeping quarters. The problem was that there was no breeze and we spent a couple of sleepless nights sweltering in our sweat-laden sheets.

It was with great relief that we lifted off the water and set course for the entrance to the Gulf of Oman. Dick passed up a chit with the course and ETA with a warning to keep a lookout for a spot height of 11,000 feet. Since we had flying conditions that were clear and unlimited visibility, or CAVU as the met. officer had described at the briefing, there was no likelihood that we would miss seeing the mountain and we levelled off at 5,000 feet and settled down to enjoy the changing panorama of the coastlines of Baluchistan and Afghanistan. The rock formations created the illusion of city skylines, with skyscrapers, spires, and towers that formed a wall on our port side that extended for hundreds of miles. I was admiring the beauty of the coast line when I was jolted out of my reverie by some more bad news from the flight engineer.

"We seem to have developed a fuel leak, just where the mainplane is attached to the hull. There's quite a distinct smell and I'd recommend we adopt a no smoking drill for the rest of the flight."

It was the usual routine on operational flights to permit the crew to smoke in the blisters and in the cockpit. I enjoyed the luxury of a pipe occasionally, but I realised the wisdom of Frank's caution. I handed control over to Don and went back aft to the blister compartment to see for myself. Just as Frank had reported, there was a tell-tale trickle of greenish aviation fuel being whipped off the trailing edge of the mainplane, and I thought I could see the origin of the leak at the upper end of the strut that braced the wing to the hull—in a location that suspiciously looked as though it had something to do with the work that was carried out at Kaferit. The leak was not serious enough to affect our safe arrival at Karachi, but it did raise fears in my mind for the prospect of further delays.

Bounnd for India

My fears were confirmed when the aircraft had been hauled from the water and on to the concrete hard standing. The squadron engineering officer shook his head after his inspection and offered his opinion.

"I'm afraid we'll have to remove the main plane again. It looks as though the leak originates in the seal between the fuel tanks and the lines that connect the fuel cocks to the engine nacelles. We're desperately short-handed and I would appreciate the assistance of your whole crew to get the job done as soon as possible. I expect you're anxious to join your squadron in Madras, but it's still going to take us five or six weeks."

We had already been three months en route and it was true that we were all anxious to get to Madras and start flying our aircraft in a useful capacity, but there was no sense in ignoring the facts. The harder we worked, the sooner we'd be on our way again. I reported to the station adjutant and he did his best to make us feel at home.

"I'll put you in quarters near your aircraft so you won't waste time getting to work. I'll have the Mess Secretary send you over some candidates for your personal bearer. Choose whichever one you like, but for goodness sake don't pay him more than twenty-five rupees a month. You'll get a hard-lying allowance while you're here because our quarters aren't really up to snuff, but you won't have much to spend your money on."

We hadn't the faintest idea what we should be looking for in a personal bearer. None of us had much experience with servants, save for the batmen and batwomen that had been assigned to us in England, who were uniformed and serving airmen and airwomen. The motley collection of candidates sent over for our selection stood respectfully before us, clutching their letters of reference from previous employees. Some of these letters dated back to the 1920s and had been beautifully written by some memsahib in elegant copperplate. In the end, I blindly chose a short, swarthy Madrasi called Mari, solely on the grounds that his English was good and he carried himself with a certain air of confidence and self-assurance.

It was something of a shock to awaken the next morning to discover my face covered with lather and a cut-throat razor being wielded by Mari within a few inches of my nose.

"*Char-lo, sahib,*" he grinned, and lifted a huge china mug from the floor where he was sitting cross-legged by my camp bed.

I took a tentative sip of the hot sweet liquid and then swallowed several appreciative gulps before cautioning Mari to leave my embryo and whispy moustache intact, a recent acquisition I had affected with the conviction that it gave me some air of authority, if not distinction. It took very little time for Mari to complete his very skilful shaving operation and to administer a steaming hot towel to my face and then with a supplicating hand-clasp to lead me to the small bathroom where a galvanised iron hip bath was brimming over with tepid water. No sooner had I seated myself in the tub than Mari began gently washing my back and lathering and rinsing my hair with an enormous sponge. When he'd finished bathing me, he had me step out on to the tiled floor and patted me dry with a large bath towel. To round off this very personal service he rubbed copious quantities of talcum powder on to my back and led me to my room where he had laid out fresh linen and clean khaki shorts and shirt. To complete my dressing he brought my service shoes freshly shined and salaamed once more before leaving.

By the time I reached the mess, Mari was waiting attentively behind a chair which he moved under me as I took my place at the table.

"Coffee, sahib?" he murmured, and filled my cup when I nodded.

I had been brought up on a diet of Rudyard Kipling at school, so I had some idea of what life was like under the British Raj, yet nothing had prepared me for that special relationship that existed between an officer and his personal bearer. Mari not only saw to my every waking need in my quarters and in the mess, but he also acted as my agent in dealing with the *dobi-wallah* and the *derzi-wallah,* and negotiated on my behalf when I made purchases in the shops along Elphinstone Street in Karachi. We had long conversations at the end of the working day, and before I walked over to the mess for dinner. He was only a few years older than me, but I learned that he had two wives and six children. When he saw Betty's picture on my night table he was surprised when I told him she was my one and only wife. He admired my cherrywood pipe, a gift from Johnny, and gave me a fill of his own tobacco, which I later discovered to be liberally mixed with hashish—as I sat on the verandah and watched the sun set, and rise, and set, and rise. When it was eventually time for us to leave for Madras it was extremely difficult to have to explain to Mari that we were unable to take him with us. I am sure that he had expected me to remain at Karachi until the end of my overseas tour, and it was with a genuine feeling of losing a close friend that I had to leave him behind.

The work on the aircraft proceeded slowly and the ground crews worked in great discomfort in the heat of the sun. For a mechanic to work inside the hull we had to be alert for signs of heat exhaustion and be ready to carry him out if he fainted. The crews worked from eight-thirty to twelve-thirty, then took a break until three in the afternoon, and worked until supper-time at six-thirty. Every piece of metal was hot to touch and tools that were left exposed to the sun became uncomfortable to handle. Before the mainplane could be removed an elaborate scaffolding of trestles had to be placed under the wing for the men to stand on. The squadron maintenance officer had to keep his own aircraft in the air and could ill-afford to deplete his work force. We made steady progress and the task was completed in the time allotted. Even so it was well into the month of July before FP252 was ready for air testing.

Finally, we were ready for the next and ultimate leg of our trip, the flight across the Indian continent to Madras. At first light, in the coolest part of the day, we loaded our gear aboard, together with some spares destined for our new squadron and an extra passenger, a Belgian civilian, who was apparently on some sort of secret mission to Burma. The flying boat base at Korangi Creek extended for three miles along one of the branches of the delta of the Indus River, whose surface waters were muddy and still. In order for the take-off run to be kept to a minimum and to allow us to get the hull to ride up on the step as soon as possible, the marine craft section sent one of its pinnaces out to ruffle the surface of the water. Even with this help, it was only by rocking the yoke back and forward gently that I was able to break the surface friction and get the aircraft planing across the creek with the nose down sufficiently to gain take-off speed. At maximum permissible power we just managed to clear the sand bar at the entrance to the anchorage with a few feet to spare, after a take-off run that lasted almost three minutes. Another few seconds and I would have had to abort the take-off.

Our track took us over the Central Deccan to a point on the southwest coast of India at Vizagapatam, about 100 miles north of Redhills Lake, a freshwater reservoir that supplied Madras with its drinking water. After crossing the coast we headed south and approached the lake from the seaward side, and close to an RAF base at St. Michael's Mount. We could see aircraft dispersed around the perimeter, Liberator bombers and Thunderbolt fighters, and it reminded us that the Japanese occupied the Andaman Islands just a few hundred miles across the Bay of Bengal. Every flight we made from now on would count toward our operational tour and we were anxious to get on with the job that we had trained for and had been ready to carry out for nearly a year.

As we flew over Redhills Lake at a steady 1,000 feet, I called Air Traffic Control for permission to land and for directions to our mooring buoy. Again the surface of the water was unbroken save for the wake of the duty pinnace, and I decided to play safe and make a powered approach to the alighting area. We had been warned that attempting glide landings in a flat calm had resulted in disaster when a pilot had been unable to judge his height above water and had flown straight into the mirror-like surface of the lake.

I was conscious that our arrival would be watched by many pairs of eyes, including those of my new squadron commander. As we approached the mooring area I made sure that the crew were all ready to make a good impression and it was only after Mick had safely wrapped the end of the short strop to the aircraft's snubbing post that I signalled STOP ENGINES.

A truck was waiting to take us from the flight area to the living quarters at the other end of the lake. The final leg of the flight was not that long by comparison to the flight from Gibraltar to Cairo, in fact only ten hours. But the accumulated wear and tear of the long delays and the frustration of the many maintenance problems that had plagued the trip, to say nothing of the guilt I still felt over the unnecessary damage to the float at Tobruk, suddenly made me feel tired.

By the time that we had found our quarters, a collection of bamboo huts on the edge of the lake, unpacked our kit and assembled the various bits of our camp gear, it was time for the evening meal. The adjutant had briefed us on the dress for dinner: khaki slacks, white shirt or long-sleeved bush jacket, and mosquito boots tied over the trousers at calf height. He warned us to use the mosquito netting provided and to be wary of snakes.

This latter remark made us a little anxious until we met George and Georgina, a family of mongooses that had free run of the bar and the dining room. One of the old hands assured us that there would be no snakes in the mess area as long as those two were around and as we sat and sipped our gins after dinner we gradually relaxed and began to feel at home.

We learned that when we were not assigned to flying operations it was the custom to sit on the verandah of the mess and watch the lofty towers of cumulus clouds build over the Bay of Bengal, signalling the onset of the monsoon season. We were entertained on such occasions by the gyrations of chameleons and small lizards that swarmed up the roof posts, and by the busy work of the armies of ants that acted as pallbearers should a small reptile expire and need to be buried.

Early next morning I reported to the squadron commander's office and handed over the chit that bore my orders.

"We'd very much like to fly FP252 as our aircraft if possible, sir. We've got quite used to her."

"That wreck? We're going to cannibalise her for spares!"

We flew several different Catalinas during the next three weeks while we were undergoing an intensive period of training before being sent out on an operational flight. Special emphasis was placed on low-level bombing and gunnery practice, as well as night flying. Once the sun goes down in the tropics conditions for the crew improve. There is less turbulence and the interior cabin temperature becomes more bearable. For the most part we flew in shorts and short-sleeved shirts and found that we could reduce the effects of prickly heat rash by using copious quantities of Johnson's baby powder, especially on the body parts that tend to produce more sweat. The waist band was particularly susceptible to excessive perspiration, a condition that was exacerbated by the need to wear a life-saving vest at all times.

However, the beginning of August marked the onset of the monsoon season and the beginning of our operational flying over the Bay of Bengal. Most of our flying was at night, through a series of cyclonic systems that brought low cloud, poor visibility, and torrential rain whipped by hurricane force winds.

Conditions in the pilot's cockpit were bad enough, but the crew, and especially Dick, our navigator, had to carry out their duties in the main cabin with no view of the outside, being tossed about by the aircraft's behaviour in the midst of violent turbulence. The Catalina was difficult to fly smoothly at our usual patrol speed of eighty-three knots, but under monsoon conditions the autopilot was just not up to coping with the rough air and we were compelled to fly manually for long hours at a stretch, with the aircraft pitching, yawing, and rolling all at the same time. Since our normal patrol was of fifteen hours' duration, we were inevitably drained physically and mentally by the end of each flight.

Most of our flights were designed to give escort to the convoys which plied up and down the east coast of India from Calcutta to Ceylon, but occasionally we were required to gather weather information from the area to the east of the Andaman Islands, which were occupied by Japanese forces. We felt particularly vulnerable as we had to take temperature and humidity readings at every thousand feet from the surface of the ocean to 10,000 feet. Our rate of climb was such that it took us almost an hour to reach that height and it was necessary to keep a good visual watch for Japanese fighters that we knew would be scrambled as soon as our aircraft had registered on the enemy radar displays. With these thoughts in mind it was comforting to know that, although we were operating a lumbering reconnaissance machine, the monsoon weather was protecting us from being intercepted by the enemy, who were equipped with faster and more heavily armed aircraft than ours.

One of the more enjoyable tasks we were given was to fly from an advance base in the Maldive Islands, which were about 300 miles south of Ceylon. The flight from Madras to Kelai took about nine hours and the first part of the flight was generally flown in darkness to take advantage of the cooler air. Kelai is a small coral atoll a little over a mile long and not quite a mile wide with an outer reef that encircles a lagoon of the clearest blue water you can imagine. In 1944 there were few facilities in the Maldives, save for a cache of fuel drums that was stacked along the beach. There were no navigational aids and Dick rose to the challenge of using dead-reckoning, supplemented by the occasional sun sight taken as we approached the latitude of the island. On Kelai itself a small base party consisting of a corporal and half a dozen ground crew lived in tents under the palms beside the sandy, windswept beach.

Apart from the infrequent arrival of flying boats that dropped in to refuel and to anchor in the lagoon, these men had no contact with the outside world other than from a wireless transmitter and the twice a year visit from a supply ship. They were all burnt a deep mahogany colour and the corporal reminded me of the character in Robert Louis Stevenson's "Treasure Island," Ben Gunn, who had been marooned by Captain Flint, and who wanted more than anything else a piece of fresh cheese. We made a point of carrying a supply of fresh fruit for them to vary the monotonous diet of canned rations and coconuts. Seeing how well they held up against the months of isolation made us all grateful for the free-wheeling lives we led, and of the independence and freedom of action we enjoyed.

We flew back from Kelai to our base through an intense cyclone associated with the onset of monsoon weather. Our task was to carry out an anti-submarine patrol, which meant flying below a cloud base that varied from 500 to 300 feet above the sea. The base of the stratus cloud was torn by a scud roll that created extremely turbulent flying conditions and made for an uncomfortable flight for the crew. Everything moveable had to be lashed down and movement within the main cabin had to be kept to a minimum.

Ron Smith, our lanky wireless operator, received a nasty

gash on the head when he was thrown against the underside of the engineer's seat as he moved forward to take his watch on the radio. The two gunners in the waist position were both stricken with air sickness and took turns vomiting into the chemical toilet until they were too exhausted to keep a visual lookout. I looked across at the second pilot and, seeing how hard he was fighting to keep from being sick, I handed over the controls to give him something to concentrate on. After watching him battle with the wheel I felt confident enough to leave the cockpit.

"I'm going to check with Dick to see how long this weather will last and see if we can't get around the eye of the storm. Keep her steady on 030 degrees and I'll get back as soon as I can."

It always amazed me that our navigator could be an oasis of calm in the midst of such foul weather. He was crouched over his chart working out the effect the shifting winds were having on our course. He looked up with a grin as though everything were normal and took up his eraser to clean up an imaginary pencil smudge in his navigation log.

"Soon be passing through the eye of the storm and we should go through a patch of calmer air in about three minutes, and I'll give you a new course to steer and an ETA for our arrival at base as soon as I've plotted this last drift sight. We should make landfall north of Madras with plenty of daylight left."

I returned to my seat but left Don to continue at the wheel so that I could save my energies for the landing. Redhills Lake was eleven miles inland, but the weather system was forecast to lie across the coast just before dusk and I was uncertain how the winds would affect landing conditions. By the time Dick had handed up our new course the turbulence had decreased appreciably, and as we neared the coastline there were breaks in the cloud masses ahead and shafts of sunlight changed the surface of the sea from a muddy green to an azure blue. I looked across at Don and caught his eye. His face had lost some of its pallor and he was able to return a weak grin.

"I have control, Don. Let's get ready for landing. Make sure we have the right recognition signals loaded in the Very pistol—don't want to invite an unwelcome greeting from the shore batteries. "

Early in September 1944, a strange Catalina arrived at Redhills, piloted by a Squadron Leader Robinson. Instead of carrying the usual load of six depth charges, his aircraft carried three DCs on the port bomb racks and only two under the starboard wing. Outboard of these was a streamlined cylinder about two and a half times the diameter of a 250 lb. depth charge with a clear perspex nose dome that housed a powerful searchlight. On top of the hull, and just aft of the pilots' cockpit, a mysterious black pear-shaped dome concealed a sophisticated radar scanner. There were more surprises within the hull: a bank of twenty-four batteries, together with an alternator, were mounted in racks under the navigator's table; on the opposite side of the main cabin, next to the wireless operator's seat, a new cathode ray display screen was mounted; and just forward of the pilots' cockpit there was a new addition in the bomb aimer's position that looked like the handlebars of a bicycle below which was a new low-level bombsight.

Squadron leader Robinson's aircraft was one of the first flying boats to be equipped with the Leigh Light (named after its inventor, Wing Commander Leigh), designed to hunt down U-boats operating at night. His task was to introduce Coastal Command crews to the technologies that had been developed to counter the new U-boat tactics. By the end of 1943, more and more U-boats were being equipped with Schnorkel breathing tubes, which enabled their captains to run at higher speed on diesel power at periscope depth, instead of running on their slower electric propulsion.

I was selected, together with another newly arrived captain, to fly with Squadron Leader Robinson and his crew to observe the new anti-submarine attack techniques. It was evident from the outset that this system could pick up small targets at a greater distance than hitherto. There was also the element of surprise that resulted from a night attack. Immediately a target was picked up on radar, the captain reduced height to 700 feet, to avoid the possibility of being picked up by the U-boat's radar. From this point on the captain concentrated on flying on instruments and listened to the voice of the radar operator, who would call out the target's range and bearing in a continuous patter. Meantime, the navigator would hand the wireless operator a position signal and then move forward to the front turret. Here, he plugged in his intercom, listened to the radar operator's patter, and prepared to manipulate the searchlight controls. At four miles range, the captain reduced height to 200 feet above the sea, using the newly installed radar altimeter to maintain a safe height, and at half a mile range the navigator switched on the searchlight and directed his attention to the low-level bombsight. When the target's speed matched that of a moving graticule of lines in his eye-piece, he released the depth charges. At this point, the captain being temporarily blinded by the glare of the searchlight, the co-pilot took over the controls and put the aircraft into a maximum climb and prepared to evade enemy fire. The attack drill called for a high degree of crew co-operation and absolute discipline in keeping all extraneous chatter off the intercom circuit.

Shortly after my introduction into the techniques and tactics of Leigh Light operations, Squadron Leader Robinson and his crew were carrying out a night shipping sweep along the convoy lane that ran from Calcutta to Madras and Ceylon. Just off coast near Vizagapatam his radar operator picked up a blip on his cathode ray screen that looked like a submarine following a convoy. Immediately, Robinson went into the attack mode and dropped his aircraft down to 200 feet for the bomb run. At the half mile point his navigator switched on the light and illuminated an American tanker that had lagged behind the convoy. Before he had time to give the order to douse the light, the tanker opened fire with its forty millimeter cannon, knocked out the lamp, scored several hits on the hull and landed a high explosive shell on the bomb-aimer's window. The luckless navigator, having realised that they were attacking a friendly ship, had turned round and was creeping back on all fours when the shell struck, peppering his buttocks with shrapnel and glass.

Robinson broke off the attack and climbed away on a course for Madras and asked the crew to report damage. It was soon evident that the hull was holed in so many places below the water line that the aircraft would probably sink on landing, even if the the whole aircraft did not break up. There was such extensive damage to the starboard wing and engine, which was losing oil rapidly, that he decided to jettison his depth charges and return to base on one engine.

We were preparing to take off at first light and received instructions to stay clear of the flare-path until the damaged aircraft had landed. My co-pilot had his own 16mm camera loaded with film and captured Robinson's skilful landing, his high speed taxi toward the shore and his subsequent safe arrival on the soft sandy beach. When we landed on our return some twelve hours later, we walked by the beached aircraft and saw for ourselves that the hull had been so peppered with light anti-aircraft fire from the tanker that it resembled a colander. Dick stopped at the sick bay, where his fellow navigator was stoically lying face down on his cot while the medical officer removed seventy-two fragments of metal and glass from his nether regions.

I'm afraid I was not so stoic when I came down with a sudden attack of dengue fever that laid me low for a week and kept the crew from flying. On my release from sick quarters I was called into the squadron commander's office and informed that my crew had been selected for Leigh Light training and were to return to Killadeas, Northern Ireland.

Meanwhile, in Europe, the Allies had landed in Normandy, Caen was captured, and the German ground forces were stubbornly preparing for a counter-offensive that would sweep the invading forces into the sea. As we boarded the train for Bombay we had mixed feelings. We were loath to leave the squadron, but we were eager to learn new operational techniques that would increase our efficiency and ultimately lead to a shortening of the war.

Our arrival in Bombay was anti-climatic. We were shown into the officers' quarters at a large transit camp at Worli, where we were confined until our ship was ready for loading. There, we discovered that a thousand double-tier bunks had been set up in a large gymnasium. This vast space was empty, save for a couple of American officers who occupied one corner of the gym, and who played the same record on a squawky record player. We settled into bunks in the opposite corner of the room and tried hard to wait patiently.

We read, we played bridge, we slept, but ever in the background was the dreamy sound of the Mills Brothers singing "Paper Doll," or "The A-Train."

Even now I associate those two tunes with seven days of enforced inactivity while the Allies were vigorously struggling to end the war in Europe.

Once aboard the troopship, however, life returned to a semblance of order. Our crew was assigned one of the turret-mounted Oerlikon cannon positions and we passed the next three weeks on look-out duties, standing two four-hour watches day and night for the whole of the fourteen-day voyage. Our passage through the Suez Canal and the Mediterranean was uneventful, but as we steamed north from Gibraltar we were reminded that the struggle for Europe was still very much on. Shipboard routine was tightened, blackout strictly enforced, and the convoy was continuously escorted by aircraft.

We arrived off Liverpool in a thick fog and crept slowly up the Mersey until we reached our berth. The city looked even dingier than it did when last I passed through in July of 1941. It was not only the drabness of the Royal Liver Building, but also the bomb damage that was evident in the districts surrounding the docks. It was obvious that Liverpool had been a prime target for the Luftwaffe's bombing raids, and row upon row of terraced homes showed irregular gaps, like a mouth with so many broken or missing teeth.

As our train pulled into Liverpool Street Station, we saw how that same broken down atmosphere existed in London. The people were tired after five years of deprivation, the rationing, the air raids, and the deaths of so many friends, neighbours, and family members. It wasn't that spirits had been broken, but that everyone was tired of the war. While there was a feeling of relief that the tide had begun to turn with the Allied landings in France, there was no longer that boisterous optimism of September 1939 when people thought the war would be over by Christmas. It was as though everybody understood that things had to get a lot worse before they would get better.

By contrast, my two weeks disembarkation leave in Devon was spent in an atmosphere of hope and a belief in ultimate victory. My brother-in-law, Doug, had come safely through the hard-fought Italian campaign and was expected home within a few months. Although rationing was still a fact of life, its effect was softened by the appearance in the shops of home-grown foods.

Betty was living at home with her parents and had returned to her work as a buyer for John Bedford's department store. I arrived home just too late to celebrate our first wedding anniversary, but her employer was understanding and generous in allowing her to take time off whilst I was on leave. We talked about the next few months and decided that as soon as I had completed the course she would join me if possible wherever I was posted. We also talked about starting a family, although the thought of parenthood seemed a little premature to me with the prospect of the war's continuing for another year or more. We also had to deal with the problem of housing when the time arrived because it was obvious that we could not continue to stay with Betty's family if we were to have a child and I were to seek a career outside the Royal Air Force.

These and other weighty issues seemed to occupy our time together and I must confess it was with some relief that I returned to my squadron duties with only one priority in mind: to finish this bloody war. I began to understand the significance of Francis Bacon's essay *Of Marriage and Single Life:* "He that hath a wife and children hath given hostages to fortune; for they are impediments to great enterprises, either of virtue or mischief."

FIFTEEN

Battle of the Atlantic
(Part II)

THE CREW THAT RETURNED to Killadeas, on Lough Erne, for Leigh Light training was vastly different from the one that had first flown together a year earlier. We had seen a great deal more of the world for one thing, and we had acquired a knowledge of each other's strengths and weaknesses, and had developed a trust in our ability to respond to any emergency. For my part I was happy to be in command of this team of specialists who brought their own individual way of responding to my orders. We had developed an easy camaraderie and an understanding of the need for a professional approach to our work. While thay addressed me as 'Skipper' at all times, we found it easy to relax in the informality of off-duty occasions and one could sense the gentle regard we had for each other. It was not always the case in other crews and I was glad that we could think of each other as friends.

The first two weeks of our course were devoted to theoretical matters and were largely composed of lectures dealing with the technical details of this new type of anti-submarine warfare, and drills that stressed the need for a high level of crew cooperation. Much of our discussions revolved around the differences between day and night attacks on U-boats.

(Back) Sgt. Sleigh, Sgt. McDougall, Sgt. Holding, Sgt. Hodgson, Sgt. Smith (Front) Sgt. Tunney, F/L Robertson, F/O Plastow, F/O Bayliss.

When we started our practical training, it was at first a matter of repeating the various drills: homing on a target with the radar operator's having complete control of the early stages of the attack; the pilot's ability to fly at low altitude in the dark, relying on the accuracy of blind flying instruments with implicit trust in the radar altimeter; and the transition of control when the navigator guided the pilot on the bombing run and operated the Leigh Light controls. When we had mastered the new attack technique we then started to inject our own improvements that would improve our timing and response to each other's roles. The co-pilot's task was to take over control after the attack when the pilot had shifted from flying on instruments to visual control when the target had been illuminated. This meant that Don had little to do in the early stages of the attack and he developed a unique system for recording the results photographically.

In a daylight attack, a series of still photographs were taken after the depth charges had been dropped and generally showed how close the explosions were to the U-boat, provided that the submarine had not crash-dived and disappeared from sight. At night, the problems were different. Some means to illuminate the target were needed, as well as a system of exposing the film at the precise moment when the depth charges exploded. Don rigged up a makeshift system which fired off a Very light with a photoflash charge in place of the usual coloured two star identification, then arranged for the camera to open its shutter at the moment the photoflash went off.

We said nothing about this to our instructors, but when we returned from a low-level bombing practice on Innishmurray Rock we were able to produce a clear photograph of our two practice bombs exploding on either side of the radar target. Subsequently, this system devised by Don was refined and adopted throughout the squadron.

By the middle of January 1945 our crew had achieved a better than average standard on the course and we were posted back to 202 Squadron, which had now moved from Gibraltar to the other end of Lough Erne, at Castle Archdale.

Not only was it a pleasure to meet former friends like my old skipper, Brian Tait, who was now a senior captain, but it was also good to be received by the two flight commanders, Squadron Leaders Mallinson and Brian Inglis, not as a junior second pilot but as a seasoned captain. My first flight as captain with 202 Squadron was a flight commander's check with Squadron Leader Inglis.

Brian was a quiet, thoughtful man, a journalist in peace time, who had established a reputation as a dependable leader and a first-rate flying boat pilot. When our check flight was over, he and I went ashore while the rest of the crew secured the aircraft at the moorings. After he had got his pipe going to his satisfaction, he spoke of the change in tactics that had altered the way in which we carried out our role in Coastal Command, and of the difficulties that we faced now that the tide of battle was changing in the Atlantic.

"You know, Robbie, our job is getting to be more difficult. The aircraft are getting older, many of our crews are in their second or third operational tour, and we are all getting tired. It's no easy task to keep alert when the chances are that most of us will never see a U-boat in a thousand hours of flying. It's hard to maintain a vigilant watch when the sky and the sea are empty for the most part and it's understandable that boredom sets in." He sucked at his pipe and gazed out over the dark waters of Lough Erne before continuing. "But we haven't won the battle yet, not by a long chalk. The U-boats are getting harder to spot and we must ensure that every sighting results in a successful attack."

Although the odds were changing in favour of the Allies, the Battle of the Atlantic was far from over. Convoys were still being attacked by day and night, ships were being sunk, and lives were being lost. To add to the misery of the Merchant Navy, the winter of 1944/45 was worse than usual.

On our first operational flight in early March, we had to return from a patrol with engine trouble, and on our second, bad weather forced our early return.

These aborted sorties had a negative affect on our morale. We began to feel guilty that we had in some way let down the seamen manning the convoy ships, and there were subtle indications that cracks were beginning to show in our *esprit de corps*. Even Dick, our pillar of strength, began to berate himself for minor errors of navigation caused by unexpected changes in the weather.

The average duration of our flights was from sixteen to eighteen hours, which meant that, including briefing and debriefing, we were on alert for twenty-four hours at a time. Dick was the only member of the crew who did not get some sort of break when he was not working over his charts, taking drift sights, or meticulously completing his log. At times, his grey-blue eyes clouded with frustration as he tried to resolve some discrepancy or fretted over his inability to be absolutely certain of our position. I tried to reassure him that there were many factors that made accurate navigation over the Atlantic diffi-cult, if not impossible. Our weather forecasting system de-pended on a few weather ships that were stationed far from land, and we had only just been equipped with navigational aids such as Gee and Loran—whose usefulness were restricted to a limited range from the coast line. Out in the middle of the Atlantic there were no aids to navigation and radio silence was still strictly enforced.

Thankfully, there had been a number of advances in our ca-pability for hunting down and attacking U-boats. The Royal Navy escort vessels were equipped with more sophisticated ra-dar and more effective fire power with their ability to fire ex-plosive missiles ahead of their ships using a multi-barrelled projectile device called a 'hedgehog.' With the arrival of newer and faster frigates the commanders of escort groups were able to take a more aggressive stance toward the hunt and, as a re-sult, the odds were beginning to turn in our favour.

Coastal Command squadrons, hitherto low priority in tech-nological advances, were now being given some useful aids in the battle against the U-boats. The new search radar, the Leigh Light, and the low-level bombsight together gave us the advan-tage of being able to surprise U-boats on the surface at night and to press home our attacks before the U-boat commanders were able to crash dive. Another advance in technology, devel-oped by our American allies, was the sonar buoy. This device consisted of buoyant canisters that were parachuted in patterns of five where a U-boat was last seen to crash dive. The buoys deployed an underwater microphone to a depth of twenty-five feet, which picked up underwater sounds such as the blowing of ballast tanks or the unmistakeable beat of electrically-driven propellers. A transmitter was automatically switched on when the buoy entered the water and its signals were sent by means of a whip antenna to aircraft within a range of seven miles. Our aircraft were fitted with a reliable Bendix radio receiver with press-button tuning that enabled us to plot the track of a submerged U-boat. In order to make the best use of these new gadgets we spent much of our off duty hours in simulators that enabled us to discriminate between underwater sounds that might be made by a riveter fish and the sounds that were caused by the mechanical systems of the U-boat.

Of course, these new tactics meant that we were for the most part flying at night in winter weather over the Atlantic and that we were either taking off or landing in the dark.

Now that I was based in Northern Ireland it became possible for Betty to join me and for us to begin to enjoy some time together. I sought, and gained (albeit somewhat grudgingly), permission to live off base and found a private hotel in the tiny village of Ballinamallard. I bought a second hand 350 cc Velocette motorcycle which enabled me to get to and from my duties at Castle Archdale. The journey was over winding country lanes and I was glad of my flying boots and fleece-lined jacket in weather that was less than clement and on roads that were often snow-bound. Fortunately, there was little traffic on the byways of war time County Fermanagh and I managed to survive those winter rides without injury or incident.

The hotel was run by a kindly lady who took us in as her only resident guests. Mrs. Crozier had a young daughter, Letitia, who brought our meals to the table and who kept a small peat fire supplied with fuel. The bathroom was just down the corridor from our bedroom and had no heating. Our room at the back of the hotel overlooked a river and we were often awoken early in the morning by a wailing cry that sounded like someone in distress. Letty told us at breakfast one morning that the cries were of a mother who was still keening after a child that had been drowned in the river five years before. Sometimes we caught a glimpse of a white-clad figure roaming up and down the river bank. It was an eery sound and we would lie awake and hold each other close for comfort. Betty was anxious to start a family and I am sure we were both thinking of the heartbreak of losing a child.

Although I was not so anxious to have children until the future seemed a little less uncertain, Betty was very concerned that there might be something that was preventing her from becoming pregnant. She argued that we had, after all, been married for fifteen months (passing lightly over the fact that I had been overseas for eleven months), and persuaded me that we seek medical advice. I asked the RAF medical officer for a referral to a specialist gynaecologist/obstetrician in Enniskillen and we drove out to his house on a wintry January day. Dr. McKay was a giant of a man with a ruddy face and a bluff, cheery manner who ushered us into his consulting room.

"How about a glass of sherry to warm us all up before we get down to business? I'd guess Tio Pepi for the young warrior, and an Amontillado for his lovely lady."

I suppose his intent was to make us feel relaxed while discussing matters of personal intimacy, but the wine merely made us more nervous, and after listening to us babbling furiously for fifteen minutes he held up his hands and laughed until I thought he would cry.

"Good gracious, my children, you've hardly been given a chance to be together long enough for anything to happen. I'll tell you what to do. Stop worrying. Go home and make love as often as you like. And have a good time. You don't know how lucky you are. Now off you go."

That was it. No medical opinion. No physical examination. No fee. Just an admonishment to go away and enjoy ourselves. It must have been effective psychology because within a couple of months Betty announced that our first child was expected in the following January.

It seems ludicrous when I look back on the incident that we were so naive, but it is merely a reflection on the times we lived in and of the rather remote relationship between doctor and patient and of the poor communication skills exercised by both parties.

Then there was the obvious stress that we were all living under, although the word was not in common usage, nor was the condition itself openly acknowledged. The air force wives living close to Lough Erne were isolated from each other, yet seemed to be part of a bad news network that kept them informed of every incident that involved our operations, despite the fact that there were few houses that had a telephone. The Crozier Hotel had no phone, and if I wanted to get a message to Betty from the base I had to call the Royal Ulster Constabulary office and ask them to have one of their men deliver it. For example, if the weather socked in over Lough Erne while we were on patrol out in the Atlantic we might receive a wireless signal ordering us to divert and land at a flying boat base where the weather was suitable for landing, say at Stranraer in Scotland. Our wives would be left wondering and had to rely on their network for information.

Such is the nature of war that we were unaware of events happening outside our theatre of operations that were to bring the struggle in Europe to a rapid close. Suddenly, after a short period of bad weather that grounded our squadron at the end of April, it was all over. May 8, 1945, was a day of wild celebration in our little village. The village band led a procession to a hilltop at the end of Ballinamallard's one and only street, where Hitler was burned in effigy. We all followed the band back to the tune of McNamara's Band and ended up at the Crozier Hotel where we celebrated the Allied victory by consuming great quantities of black, nourishing porter ale.

U-boat flying the black flag of surrender.

Two days later our crew was carrying out a routine patrol along the Blue Line, the ten degree line of longitude west of Ireland, with the aim of intercepting any German U-boat that was obeying the terms of the armistice by travelling on the surface and flying a black flag. It was a strange feeling, when we sighted a submarine proceeding north, to have to control the urge to sound the alarm and proceed with a depth charge attack. After all, this was only the third sighting for me in four years and flying thousands of miles over the waters of the Gulf of Mexico, the Mediterranean Sea, the Indian Ocean, and the North Atlantic. Instead, I picked up the Aldis lamp and sent a signal by Q-code (an international three letter marine code), instructing the U-boat commander to set course for Loch Eriboll in the north of Scotland. We transmitted the position of our prisoner and escorted him until we had reached our endurance and had been relieved by another Catalina.

A few days later we were one of two crews from our squadron who travelled by road to Londonderry, where three other

U-boats were berthed and in the hands of a Royal Navy prize crew, guarded by a company from the Green Howard Regiment. As we crawled through the hull of one of the surrendered submarines we were all affected by feelings of sympathy with the German crews who lived in such cramped quarters and suffered the privations of long Atlantic patrols. Up to now they had been the faceless enemy. Now we were brought into contact with the facts of their everyday lives. For the first time, the enemy, we realised, were individual human beings. Their faces were not unlike those of my own crew, who had fought together for two long years. We had come to rely on each other as they had, and, looking around at the weary faces of my own crew, I could see the cumulative effects of the wear and tear of those last two years.

I flew my last patrol with 202 Squadron on May 10 and we mustered for one last time when the squadron disbanded on June 10, 1945. It was a bitter-sweet occasion, for although it was partly a victorious celebration, it was also tinged with regret that we were meeting for the last time as a family, and it was in a sense a memorial to those of our squadron who had lost their lives during the Battle of the Atlantic.

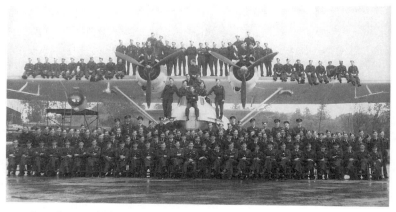

202 Squadron at disbanding in June 1945.

SIXTEEN

Return to India

MOST OF THE CAPTAINS from 202 Squadron were posted to Transport Command for troop-carrying operations designed to reinforce the ground war against the Japanese. I was ordered to report to 220 Squadron, based at St. David's in Pembrokeshire, where I was to be one of four captains undergoing conversion training to B-24 Liberator aircraft. Unfortunately, the transport crew complement consisted of captain, co-pilot, navigator, and engineer. This meant that my crew was split up. My navigator and rigger returned to Australia for demobilisation; the three WAGs were surplus to requirement and were posted to various signalling tasks in England; Don, my second pilot, was posted to an advanced flying school; and Jock, the second flight engineer, left us for a posting nearer home. Only Frank, my first engineer, accompanied me to St. David's, where he immediately became immersed in the intricacies of the Liberator petrol system, the hydraulic system, and the emergency systems. We were joined by Graham, a navigator straight out of navigators' school, and Flight Sergeant Gillatt, who became my co-pilot. By the end of June 1945 I had been declared proficient as a four-engine pilot and the new crew was given two weeks leave before starting serious training for route operations at our new base at Waterbeach, just north of Cambridge.

The whole experience of changing from flying a Catalina to piloting a B-24 converted bomber was, for me, somewhat daunting. For nearly three years I had been accustomed to taking off from and landing on the water at speeds of sixty to seventy miles an hour. Although the Catalina and the Liberator were both built by the Consolidated Company in California, they were completely different in their flying characteristics. I now had to get used to piloting the weight of a 60,000 lb aircraft, a boundary crossing speed with power on of about 130 miles an hour, and a precise point to land on the threshold of a concrete runway of finite length. In addition, a new mind set was required to fly transport aircraft with a full complement of twenty-six passengers. Flying below cloud at heights below 1,000 feet was frowned upon and flight levels were chosen more with regard to passenger comfort and favourable weather conditions than by any operational necessity.

Another change had taken place with the end of hostilities in Europe. Many of the experienced maintenance technicians were being demobilised as their term of wartime service came to an end and there was a mood of impatience in those awaiting their number to come up. As a result, standards of aircraft maintenance were not high as they had once been and we began to hear alarming stories of aircraft accidents that were caused by carelessness or a lack of enthusiasm on the part of those who were impatient to return home again, accidents that resulted in unnecessary loss of lives and aircraft.

The drop in morale was accentuated after the Japanese surrender in August 1945, and it was evident that many who had volunteered for war-time service had lost their motivation and were becoming disgruntled at having to wait their turn for demobilisation.

Early in October, I was assigned to fly to India carrying troops to reinforce the garrisons in the South East Asia Theatre of Operations. An hour's flight from Waterbeach brought us to the Melsbroek airfield near Brussels where we loaded twenty-six soldiers of the 51st Highland Division. The flight to our next staging post, Castel Benito in Tripoli, would take nearly seven hours and our flight plan was predicated on a take-off time an hour before midnight in order to land in Tripoli just after dawn.

The British troops were well-disciplined and accepted the various modes of transportation and the attendant discomforts with remarkable patience. In the converted Liberator bombers passengers were carried in two rows of facing seats in what used to be the bomb bay and there was much bawdy humour over their sitting knee to knee. I received clearance to taxi and found myself third in line for take-off with eight other aircraft behind me. The first aircraft in line received the green light and we watched it thunder off into the night with its turbo exhausts giving off great tongues of fire. It had barely become airborne when its lights disappeared and the roar of its engines was replaced by an ominous silence. For an instant I was conscious of holding my breath, then suddenly we felt the earth shudder beneath us.

The leading aircraft had crashed into a railway embankment at the end of the runway and had immediately burst into flames. I remember just having time to realise that there could be no survivors when the radio crackled in my ears.

"Exray Able, line up prepare for take-off. Exray Uncle stand by to line up and hold after Exray Able has cleared the runway."

There was no time for further thought about the fate of others and I taxied forward to the hold position as the second aircraft moved on to the runway for take-off. As soon as his lights had disappeared into the low cloud the controller's voice sounded crisply in my headphones.

"Exray Uncle, cleared for take-off."

I lined up on the runway and selected full boost on the turbos, then opened the throttle for maximum take-off power and headed off into the darkness. Two-thirds of the way down the runway we became airborne, then, as I called for 'wheels up' we flew over the burning Liberator and headed off into the night sky, relieved that all four of our engines were carrying us safely aloft.

When we returned to Waterbeach two weeks later we learned the accident that had cost thirty lives had been caused by incorrectly installed ignition harnesses and was attributed to faulty maintenance.

At Castel Benito we had an overnight stop, enjoying the comforts of a permanent airfield that had been built for the Italian Air Force, then took off with our load of troops for Cairo. At Cairo the soldiers of the 51st Highland Division were exchanged for a similar complement of Indian troops bound for Delhi. A very smart *subahdar* saluted and asked for instructions that he should pass on to his men, and I stressed the importance of remaining seated until the aircraft had reached cruising altitude, and then to keep movement restricted to necessary trips to the chemical toilet. I suggested that he occupy the seat nearest the cockpit door so that I could pass any emergency instructions to him once we were airborne.

We took off at dusk and headed for Shaibah on the Persian Gulf. For an hour all was quiet until the *subahdar* poked his head into the cockpit and shouted in my ear.

"Excuse me, Captain, but all four of our engines are on fire!"

I chuckled to myself and explained to the *subahdar* that the flames issuing from our turbo exhaust system were quite normal and that his men were safe. The view that the passengers had from the small ports in the bomb bay was restricted to the underside of the nacelles where the exhaust gases were fluttering only a few feet away.

A brief stop at Shaibur to refuel and we were off again into the darkness, bound for Karachi. Another refuelling stop gave crew and passengers a chance to stretch our legs and have a meal, then we were off to Delhi's Palam airfield where we disembarked our Indian troops.

The final leg of our outbound trip terminated at Chakulia, an airfield about 100 miles west of Calcutta that had been built by the American forces for their B-29 Superfortresses as a base for the final assault on Japan. The runways were long and wide, wide enough for a small plane to land across them, and there was ample room for a Liberator to land with runway to spare.

At Chakulia we picked up a different load of passengers, all of whom were repatriated prisoners of war who had suffered various degrees of ill-treatment, including both physical and psychological abuse from their captors.

Our new passengers were pathetically patient and grateful for any small consideration that we could offer them. We carried them by gentle stages all the way back to England and we all felt that we were ferrying a very special and precious cargo.

We left Chakulia in the middle of monsoon season and had to climb to 10,000 feet before we were flying in the clear. It was only a seven hour flight to Karachi, but we stayed overnight so that our passengers could get a good rest and receive necessary medical attention. The next leg was a tiring flight of over ten hours to Lydda in Palestine. Here we rested overnight again and took off with our Liberator laden with citrus fruits that the crew were planning to take home to our families. From Lydda to El Adem was only four hours, but we overnighted again to spare the passengers. The airfield was in the middle of the Libyan desert and the accommodation was primitive, consisting of a small scattering of tents and a limited supply of fresh water. Our passengers showed remarkable forebearance and there was no word of complaint from them and certainly none from us.

Another four-hour flight took us to Castel Benito, where we knew the accommodation to be first-class. Two of our passengers were showing signs of fatigue and the medical officer asked if we could give them an extra night's rest. The crew and I were quite happy to accede to his request and indulged ourselves in frequent tepid showers between the rubbers of bridge that had become our way of relaxing between stages. The flight from Castel Benito to Rabat Sale, near Casablanca, took over six hours and we rested again overnight before the final leg of our journey to the United Kingdom. We sensed the buzz of excitement as our passengers realised that they were nearing England and home.

The following morning we were loaded and ready for a nine o'clock take-off. The weather forecast was exquisitely simple: ceiling and visibility unlimited. We climbed to 5,000 feet and set course for Cape St. Vincent on the southern tip of the Iberian Peninsular. The automatic pilot was behaving well and the Liberator flew steadily through calm skies.

Suddenly, and without warning, the revolutions of the number two engine started to fluctuate wildly and increased to the point where I was forced to feather the propeller before it tore the engine nacelle from the wing. We were six and a half hours from home and our route was for the most part over water. I knew that the Liberator could fly quite comfortably on three engines, but my decision was clear. The safety of the passengers came first and I turned the plane around and headed back to Rabat.

On landing at Rabat I addressed the passengers and apologised for the extra day's delay in getting them home. I could see the disappointment in their faces, but they were very understanding and shrugged the incident off without complaint.

The next day we flew up the coast of Spain and Portugal, the scene of so many of my patrols from Gibraltar, and crossed the Bay of Biscay where I recalled earlier times when we would have had to be on the lookout for marauding squadrons of Junkers 88's that preyed upon slower reconnaissance planes.

This was not to be my last contact with expatriot prisoners of war, nor my last dealings with German prisoners, for I found on my return to the squadron office that I had been transferred to command a transit camp at Bourn, west of Cambridge on the road to Huntington. The camp was staffed by a small cadre of RAF personnel who supervised the work of prisoners of war from all branches of the German miltary services. It was ironic that the transit camp existed for the sole purpose of processing British ex-prisoners of war such as our former passengers. It took on average about five working days to pass them through medical inspections, arrange for them to receive their back pay, and to make up any deficiencies in their uniforms and equipment. At the conclusion of this, for them, tiresome procedure, they were sent off on four weeks' leave before demobilisation or assignment to new duties.

I missed the flying, but quite enjoyed the change of routine. I had the luxury of personal transport in the shape of a 500 cc Norton motorcycle and sidecar, to enable me to carry out the varied duties that came my way: as President of the Transit Officers' Mess I was responsible for picking up weekly supplies of beer and liquor, cigarettes, and chocolate for the members; inspecting the prisoner-of-war lines with their senior officer, at that time a former U-boat commander; and attending to the needs of our own RAF personnel. It was, I imagined, rather like being the mayor of a small town who has to be concerned with everything from road repair to the collection of garbage and the provision of a variety of social services. I was fortunate to have an experienced Station Warrant Officer who dealt with the myriad of administrative details and the promulgation of Station Standing Orders.

My work was time-consuming, but mainly decorative. I had to be available to answer queries from primary clients, the repatriated Allied prisoners of war that were our guests for a week or so. I was in charge of the weekly church parades for a population of 500 and enjoyed a rather unique relationship with the three chaplains that tended our separate flocks: Church of England, Roman Catholic, and a small Jewish contingent.

About this time I was faced with a decision that would affect the rest of my life. An offer of an extended service commission was open to all General Duties officers until the end of May 1946. I discussed the pros and cons of the offer with Betty and we finally decided that I should opt for a career in teaching as soon as my turn for mobilisation came up. With lightning rapidity it was all over. I received notification that I was to report to RAF Station, Hendon, for demobilisation on 31 July, 1946. I handed in my airforce equipment and in return was issued with an outfit of civilian clothes, a civilian ration book, the balance of my pay, and a travel warrant to take me home to a new life as a school teacher.

Years later, I found a book of Ronald Searle's sketches from prison camp in 1939–1945, which he calls "the *graffiti* of a condemned man, intending to leave a rough witness of his passing through, but who found himself—to his surprise and delight—among the reprieved." Although our experiences were different, I can empathise with his feelings. Hence these personal memoirs.

Afterword

IN WRITING DOWN THIS ACCOUNT of my six years of war I was able to recall incidents and individuals with the utmost clarity, which is rather surprising since I am now sometimes unable to remember what I had for lunch yesterday. It reminds me of a line in the film "The Three Days of the Condor," in which a young CIA agent asks his chief (played by John Houseman, the master of the double take) what it was like during WW II and what made the times different. John Houseman takes the longest time to consider the question, looks away, then back again with a long pause before answering: "The clarity."

Those of my generation who survived and grew to manhood during the Second World War will understand the way small incidents are vividly recalled as though they had been illuminated by a star shell. In the same way friendships are made that endure all time. Johnny, Farmer, and I had that sort of friendship. Johnny was the first of we three to go into action and was killed over Germany even before Farmer and I graduated. He still lives in my memory, and the following poem might have been written for him:

For Johnny

Do not despair
For Johnny-head-in-air;
He sleeps as sound
As Johnny underground.

Fetch out no shroud
For Johnny-in-the-cloud;
And keep your tears
For him in after years.

Better by far
For Johnny-the-bright-star
To keep your head
And see his children fed.

—*John Pudney, "Ten Summers"* *(1944)*

Glossary

AFC	Air Force Cross
AFU	Advanced Flying Unit
Aldis	signalling lamp
ATCO	Air Traffic Control Officer
BBC	British Broadcasting Corporation
Chance Light	floodlight used for night flying
Char	slang word for tea (Hindi)
Chipmunk	training aircraft built by Dehavilland
Derzi-wallah	Indian tailor
DFC	Distinguished Flying Cross
Dhobi-wallah	washerman/woman
DSO	Distinguished Service Order
Erk	Aircraftsman 2nd Class—lowest rank in the RAF
Gippy Tummy	form of metadysentery causing diarrhea
ITW	Initial Training Wing
Jock	nickname for all Scots
Kosbies	King's Own Scottish Borderers Regiment
NAAFI	Navy, Army & Airforce Institute—service canteens
NCO	Non-commissioned officer
Nissen Hut	temporary barracks built from sections of corrugated iron, set on concrete base

OTC	Officers' Training Corps
OTU	Operational Training Unit
Poodle faking	chatting up the popsies (see below)
Popsies	attractive young women
RAAF	Royal Australian Air Force
RASC	Royal Army Service Corps, suppliers of rations to the RAF
2nd dicky	co-pilot
Sidcot suit	one-piece flying overall
Swan Vestas	popular brand of sulphur match
SWO	Station Warrant Officer
Subahdar	chief native officer of an Indian infantry company
Trots	flying boat anchorage
U-boat	German submarine (from *unterseeboot*)
U/T	under training
Very pistol	signal pistol used for identification (fired two-star cartridge)
VSI	Vertical Speed Indicator
WAAF	Women's Auxiliary Air Force
WAG	Wireless Operator Air Gunner
Walton Dinghy	tender for ferrying crews from shore to flying boat anchorage
Wimpy	Wellington bomber made by Vickers-Armstrong
WOM	Wireless Operator Mechanic
WRNS	Women's Royal Naval Service, nicknamed "wrens"

Biography

ALAN ROBERTSON was born in London in June, 1923. He attended Wilson's Grammar School in Camberwell from 1935 to 1939 and joined the RAF on New Year's Day 1941. He served as a pilot until July 1946, when he was demobilised and started teacher training at Cheltenham. Upon graduation he taught in Plymouth until 1951, when he was recalled to the RAF and trained as a flying instructor. He served on the staff at RAF Cranwell, first as a flight commander, and then as Officer Commanding Junior Entries.

On retiring from the RAF, he emigrated to Canada, where he taught, first in Saskatchewan, and then in Calgary, Alberta. He completed graduate studies in theatre at Carnegie-Mellon University and joined the faculty of the University of Calgary, where

he served from 1969 to 1987, finally retiring as Dean of Fine Arts.

He moved to Vancouver on retirement, where he enjoyed another satisfying career as actor/director, appearing on film, stage, and television until he moved to Victoria in 1998, where he is enjoying semi-retirement.